THOMAS NASHE

PIERCE PENILESSE, HIS SVPPLICATION TO THE DIVELL
(1592)

XI

BODLEY HEAD QUARTOS

THE BODLEY HEAD QUARTOS

EDITED BY G. B. HARRISON

THOMAS NASHE

PIERCE PENILESSE, HIS SVPPLICATION TO THE DIVELL (1592)

GREENWOOD PRESS, PUBLISHERS
WESTPORT, CONNECTICUT

Note

THE ORIGINAL of this text is in the British Museum (C.40.d.g). A list of the misprints which have been corrected in the text will be found on page 138.

G. B. H.

Originally published in 1924
by E. P. Dutton & Company

First Greenwood Reprinting 1970

SBN 8371-2919-2

PRINTED IN UNITED STATES OF AMERICA

INTRODUCTION

PIERCE PENILESSE HIS SVPPLICATION TO THE DIVELL was one of the most successful and popular of Elizabethan pamphlets. It was entered in the *Stationers' Register* on 8th August, 1592, and before the year was out no less than three editions were issued. It was reprinted in 1593 and again in 1595.

Nashe was a rambling and discursive writer; he wandered from subject to subject just as his pen led him, and, for that very reason, *Pierce Penilesse* with all its digressions is of considerable importance as an epitome of the many interests of Englishmen in the very anxious year 1592.

'Pierce Penilesse' begins his lamentation with the very common (and very real) complaint of the professional writer that the times are bad; now that 'gentle *Sir Philip Sidney*' is dead, there is no one left to care for poor scholars. In despair, therefore, Pierce draws up a 'Supplication to the Devil,' suggesting that if he were to remove a few of the old misers and usurers, gold would circulate more freely. He then goes to search for the Devil, but cannot find him in London—he is too busy in the North. At last, however, he meets a 'Knight of the Post' (*i.e.* a professional perjurer) who consents to deliver the letter.

Then follows the Supplication itself, which is founded on the familiar mediæval theme of the Seven Deadly Sins. Usurers lead up to Greediness and Nigardize, and so on to Pride (with an attack on Antiquarians by the way), Envy, Murder, Wrath, and railers. This gives Nashe an opportunity for a fine defence of poetry and poets against its detractors, amongst whom was to be numbered Richard Harvey and his more famous brother Gabriel, the Cambridge scholar. Pierce then returns to Gluttony, Drunkenness and Sloth, which has brought plays and players into disrepute.

Nashe's defence of plays is rightly famous: its tone is curiously modern. He claims that plays are 'a rare exercise of vertue' because they revive the glories of our ancestors, 'than which, what can be a sharper reproofe to these degenerate, effeminate days.' It is comforting to remember that these words were written just four years after the defeat of the Spanish Armada. And again, he notes the answer of 'any Collian or clubfisted Vsurer' when the glories of Henry the Fifth are mentioned—'I, but they will say, *what do we get by it?*'

Our modern 'Collians' say much the same when the question of educational expenditure is brought up.

The seventh and last evil is Lechery, and with that the Supplication proper comes to an end. Then follows a discourse between Pierce and the Knight of the Post on a question which greatly interested the Elizabethan Londoner—the nature of Hell and the Devil.[1] Spiritualistic inquiry had indeed recently received a great stimulus by events in May 1591 in Scotland,[2] where witches had been discovered plotting against the King's life. As this conversation naturally suggests the question of Demonology, Nashe inserts a long passage (pp. 96–131) directly translated from the *Isagoge* of Georgius Pictorius, in the midst of which, by way of digression, he gives an allegory of the wickedness of the Bear (the Earl of Leicester), and his friends the Fox and the Camelion (the Martinists). He then returns to the Demons and brings the book to an abrupt end with the praises of a young nobleman called 'Amyntas.'[3]

[1] Compare Faustus' conversation with Mephistophilis in Marlowe's *Faustus*.

[2] For an account of the Scottish Witch Trials, see *Newes from Scotland*, printed in vol. IX of the *Bodley Head Quartos*.

[3] Probably the young Earl of Southampton.

The story of the famous quarrel between Nashe and the Harveys is long and somewhat intricate.[1] Richard Harvey, in his *Lamb of God*, 1590, had spoken slightingly of the professional writers who were paid to answer the *Martin Marprelate* pamphlets, and in particular he had sneered at Nashe. Robert Greene, who was head of the group, retorted in his *Quip for an Vpstart Courtier* (published in July or August 1592) with an abusive paragraph about the Harvey family, which was afterwards suppressed.[2] Nashe now added a few words in *Pierce Penilesse* (p. 62). In August, the plague was violent in London, and Nashe went away. Meanwhile legal business had brought Gabriel Harvey to London. On the 3rd September Greene died, and Harvey, who was furious at the attacks made on his family, began to write his *Foure Letters*,[3] in the second of which he describes Greene's death; in the third he replies quite mildly to Nashe. Nashe immediately retorted with a bitter and scathing commentary—*Strange Newes, Of the intercepting certaine Letters*. Thereafter the combatants attacked

[1] For a full account see Dr. McKerrow's *Nashe*, vol. V, p. 65, etc.

[2] It is reprinted in my *Shakespeare's Fellows*, p. 58.

[3] Vol. II in the *Bodley Head Quartos*.

each other in a succession of scurrilous pamphlets, of which the best is Nashe's *Haue with you to Saffron-walden, or, Gabriel Harueys Hunt is vp* (1596)—one of the finest pieces of abuse in the language. However, after seven years the affair became a public nuisance, and on 1st June, 1599, the Stationers' Company were ordered to seize all books written by Harvey and Nashe and to see 'that none of theire bookes bee euer printed hereafter.'

The text of this reprint is that of the third edition of 1592, which has been chosen in preference to the first or second because it bears marks of having received the author's final corrections. The first edition, which was issued during Nashe's absence from London, has the following title-page and epistle:

Pierce Penileſse his

Supplication to the

Diuell.

Deſcribing the ouer-ſpreading of

Vice, and ſuppreſion of

Vertue.

Pleaſantly interlac'd with variable de-
lights: and pathetically intermixt
with conceipted reproofes.

Written by *Thomas Naſh* Gentleman.

[DEVICE]

LONDON,

Imprinted by *Richard Ihones*, dwelling at
the Signe of the Rose and Crowne,
nere Holburne Bridge.

1592.

The Printer to the Gentlemen
Readers.

Gentlemen:

In the Authours absence, I haue been bold to publish this pleasaunt and wittie Discourse of *Pierce Penilesse his Supplication to the Diuell:* which Title though it may seeme strange and in it selfe somewhat preposterous, yet if you vouchsafe the Reading, you shall finde reason, aswell for the Authours vncouth nomination, as for his vnwonted beginning without Epistle, Proeme, or Dedication: al which he hath inserted conceitedly in the matter; but Ile be no blab to tell you in what place. Bestow the looking, and I doubt not but you shall finde Dedication, Epistle, & Proeme to your liking.

Yours bounden in affection:

R. I.

This 'long-tayld Title' annoyed Nashe, who now added the Epistle printed on page 1 of the text, and caused the offending Title and Epistle to be removed.

I wish to express my warm thanks to Dr. R. B. McKerrow: in general for much help in the production of the *Bodley Head Quartos*, and in particular for permission to make considerable use of his five volume edition of *The Works of Thomas Nashe* in preparing this reprint for the Press.

G. B. HARRISON

Pierce Penilesse
HIS SVPPLICATION
.to the Diuell.

Barbaria grandis habere nihil.

Written by *Tho. Nash*, Gent.

LONDON,
printed by Abell Ieffes, for
I. B. 1592.

A priuate Epistle of the Author to *the Printer.*

Wherein his full meaning and purpose (in publishing this Booke) is set foorth.

FAITH I am verie sorrie (Sir) I am thus vnawares betrayed to infamie. You write to me my book is hasting to the second impression: he that hath once broke the Ice of impudence, need not care how deepe he wade in discredit. I confesse it to be a meer toy, not deseruing any iudicial mans view: If it haue found any friends, so it is, you knowe very wel that it was abroad a fortnight ere I knewe of it, & vncorrected and vnfinished, it hath offred it selfe to the open scorne of the world. Had you not beene so forward in the republishing of it, you shold haue had certayne Epistles to Orators and Poets, to insert to the later end; As namely, to the Ghost of *Macheuill*, of *Tully*, of *Ouid*, of *Roscius*, of *Pace* the Duke of Norfolks Iester; and lastly, to the Ghost of *Robert Greene*, telling him, what a coyle there is with pamphleting on him after his death. These were prepared for *Pierce Penilesse* first setting foorth, had not the feare of infection detained mee with my Lord in the Countrey.

Now this is that I woulde haue you to do in

this second edition; First, cut off that long-tayld Title, and let mee not in the forefront of my Booke, make a tedious Mountebanks Oration to the Reader, when in the whole there is nothing praise-worthie.

I heare say there bee obscure imitators, that goe about to frame a second part to it, and offer it to sell in Paules Churchyard, and elsewhere, as from mee. Let mee request you (as euer you will expect any fauour at my hands) to get some body to write an Epistle before it, ere you set it to sale againe, importing thus much; that if any such lewde deuise intrude it selfe to their hands, it is a coseanage and plaine knauery of him that sels it to get mony, and that I haue no manner of interest or acquaintance with it. Indeed if my leysure were, such as I could wish, I might haps (halfe a yeare hence) write / the returne [¶ of the *Knight of the Post* from hel, with the *Deuils* answer to the *Supplication*: but as for a second part of *Pierce Penilesse*, it is a most ridiculous rogery.

Other news I am aduertised of, that a scald triuial lying pamphlet, cald *Greens groats-worth of wit* is giuen out to be of my doing. God neuer haue care of my soule, but vtterly renoũce me, if the least word or sillable in it proceeded from my pen, or if I were any way priuie to the writing or printing of it. I am growne at length to see into the vanity of the world more than euer I did, and now I condemne my selfe for nothing so much, as playing the dolt in Print. Out vpon it, it is odious, specially, in this moralizing age, wherein euery one seeks to shew himselfe a Polititian by mis-interpreting. In one place of my Booke *Pierce Penilesse* saith, but to the Knight of the Post, *I pray how might I call you*, & they say, I meant one *Howe*, a Knaue of that trade, that I neuer heard of before. The Antiquaries are offended without cause, thinking I goe about to detract from that excellent profession, when (God is my witnesse) I reuerence it as much as any of them all, and had no manner of allusion to them that stumble at it. I hope they wil giue me leaue to think there be fooles of that Art as well as of al other; but to say I vtterly condemne it as an vnfruitfull studie, or seeme to despise the excellent qualified partes of it, is a most false and iniurious surmise. There is nothing that if a man list he may not wrest or peruert, I cannot forbid anie to thinke villainously, *Sed caueat emptor*, Let the interpreter beware: for none euer hard me make Allegories of an idle text. Write who wil against me, but let him look his life be without scandale: for if he touch me neuer so litle, Ile be as good as the Blacke Booke to him & his kindred. Beggerly lyes no beggerly wit but can inuent: who spurneth not at a dead dogge? but I am of another mettal, they shall know that I liue as their euil Angel, to haunt them world without end, if they disquiet me without cause. Farewell, and let me heare from you as soone as it is come forth. I am the Plagues prisoner in the Country as yet: if the sicknesse cease before the thirde impression, I wil come and alter whatsoeuer may be offensiue to any man, and bring you the latter ende.

Your friend, Tho. Nash. / [¶v

Pierce Penilesse his Supplication to the Diuell.

HAUING spent many yeeres in studying how to liue, and liu'de a long time without mony: hauing tired my youth with follie, and surfetted my minde with vanitie, I began at length to looke backe to repentaunce, & addresse my endeuors to prosperitie: But all in vaine, I sate vp late, and rose earely, contended with the colde, and conuersed with scarcitie: for all my labours turned to losse, my vulgar Muse was despised & neglected, my paines not regarded or slightly rewarded, and I my selfe (in prime of my best wit) laid open to pouertie. Wherevpon (in a malecontent humor) I accused my fortune, raild on my patrones, bit my pen, rent my papers, and ragde in all points like a mad man. In which agony tormenting my selfe a long time, I grew by degrees to a milder discontent: and pausing a while ouer my standish, I resolued in verse to paint forth my passion: which best agreeing with the vaine of my vnrest, I began to complaine in this sort.

Discite qui sapitis, cum hæc quæ scimus inertes: Sed trepidas acies, & fera bella sequi.

Est aliquid fatale malum, per verba leuare.

Why ist damnation to dispaire and die,
When life is my true happinesse disease?
My soule, my soule, thy safetye makes me flie
The faultie meanes, that might my paine appease.
Diuines and dying men may talke of hell,
But in my heart, her seueral tormentes dwell.
Ah worthlesse Wit, to traine me to this woe,
Deceitfull Artes that nourish Discontent:
Ill thriue the Follie that bewitcht me so, / [A1
Vaine thoughts adieu, for now I will repent.
And yet my wantes perswade me to proceede,
Since none takes pitie of a Scollers neede.
Forgiue me God, although I curse my birth,
And ban the aire, wherein I breath a Wretch:
Since Miserie hath daunted all my mirth,
And I am quite vndone through promise-breach.
Pol me occidistis amici.
Oh friends, no friends, that then vngently frowne,
When changing Fortune casts vs headlong downe.
Without redresse complaines my carelesse verse,
And Mydas-*eares relent not at my moane:*
In some far Land will I my griefes reherse,
Mongst them that will be mou'd when I shall groane.
England (*adieu*) *the Soyle that brought me foorth,*
Adieu vnkinde, where skill is nothing woorth.

These Rymes thus abruptly set downe, I tost my imaginations a thousand waies to see if I could finde any meanes to relieue my estate: But all my thoughts consorted to this conclusion, that the world was vncharitable, & I ordaind to be miserable. Thereby I grew to consider how many base men that wanted those parts which I had, enioyed content at will, and had wealth at commaund: I cald to minde a Cobler, that was worth fiue hundred pound, an Hostler that had built a goodly Inne & might dispende fortie pound yerely by his Land, a Carre-man in a lether pilche, that had whipt out a thousand pound out of his horse taile: and haue I more wit than all these (thought I to my selfe) am I better borne? am I better brought vp? yea and better fauored? and yet am I a begger? What is the cause? how am I crost? or whence is this curse?

Euen from hence, that men that should employ such as I am, are enamoured of their own wits, and thinke what euer they do is excellent, though it be neuer so scuruie: that Learning (of the ignorant) is rated after the value of the inke and paper: & a Scriuener better paid for an obligation, than a Scholler for the best Poeme he can make; that *euery grosse braind Idiot is suffered to come into

Scribimus indocti doctique poemata passim.

print, who if hee set foorth a Pamphlet of the praise of Pudding-pricks, or write a Treatise of *Tom Thumme*, or the / exployts of [A1v *Vntrusse*; it is bought vp thicke and threefold, when better things lie dead. How then can we chuse but be needy, when ther are so many Droans amongst vs? or euer proue rich that toyle a whole yeare for faire lookes? Gentle *Sir Phillip Sidney*, thou knewst what belongd to a Scholler, thou knewst what paines, what toyle, what trauel conduct to perfection: wel couldst thou giue euery Vertue his encouragement, euery Art his due, euery writer his desert: cause none more vertuous witty, or learned than thy selfe.

Heu rapiunt mala fata bonos.

But thou art dead in thy graue, and hast left too few successors of thy glory, too few to cherish the Sons of the Muses, or water those budding hopes with their plenty, which thy bounty erst planted.

Beleeue me Gentlemen, for some crosse mishapes haue taught me experience, ther is not that strict obseruation of honour, which hath beene heeretofore. Men of great calling take it of merite, to haue their names eternizde by Poets, & whatsoeuer pamphlet or dedication encounters them, they put it vp in their sleeues, and scarce giue him thankes that presents it. Much better is it for those golden

Pens, to raise such vngratfull Peasants from the Dung-hil of obscuritie, and make them equal in fame to the Worthies of olde, when their doting selfe-loue shall challenge it of dutie, and not onely giue them nothing themselues, but impouerish liberality in others.

This is the lamentable condition of our Times, that men of Arte must seeke almes of Cormorantes, and those that deserue best, be kept vnder by Dunces, who count it a policie to keepe them bare, because they should follow their bookes the better: thinking belike, that as preferment hath made themselues idle, that were earst painefull in meaner places, so it would likewise slacken the endeuours of those Students that as yet striue to excell, in hope of aduauncement. A good policy to suppresse superfluous liberalitie. But had it beene practised when they were promoted, the Yeomandry of the Realme had beene better to passe than it is, and one Droane should not haue driuen so many Bees from their hony-combes.

I, I, weele giue loosers leaue to talke, it is no matter what *Sic probo* and his pennilesse companions prate, whilest we haue / the [A2 gold in our coffers: this is it that will make a knaue an honest man, and my neighbour *Cramptons* stripling a better Gentleman than his Grandsier. O it is a trim thing, when Pride the sonne goes before, and Shame the father followes after. Such presidents there are in our Common-wealth a great many: not so much of them whome Learning and Industry hath exalted, (whom I preferre before *Genus* and *proauos*) as of Carterly vpstarts, that out-face Towne and Country in their Veluets, when Sir *Rowland Russet-coat* their Dad, goes sagging euery day in his round Gascoynes of whyte cotton, and hath much a doo (poore pennie-father) to keepe his vnthrift elbowes in reparations.

Marry happy are they (say I) that haue such fathers to worke for them whilest they play, for where other men turne ouer many leaues to get bread and cheese in their old age, and study twentie yeeres to distill golde out of inke; our young maisters doe nothing but deuise how to spend and aske counsaile of the Wine and Capons, how they may quickliest consume their patrimonies. As for me, I liue secure from all such perturbations: for (thankes be to God) I am *vacuus viator*, and care not though I meete the Commissioners of *Newmarket-heath* at high midnight, for any Crosses, Images, or Pictures that I carry about me more than needes.

Than needes (quoth I) nay I would be

ashamde of it, if *Opus* and *Vsus* were not knocking at my doore twentie times a weeke when I am not within; the more is the pittie, that such a franke Gentleman as I, should want: but since the dice do runne so vntowardly on my side, I am partly prouided of a remedie. For whereas those that stand most on their honour, haue shut vp their purses, and shifte vs off with court-holie-bread: and on the other side, a number of hypocriticall hot-spurres, that haue God alwayes in their mouthes, will giue nothing for Gods sake; I haue clapt vp a handsome Supplication to the Diuell, and sent it by a good fellow, that I know will deliuer it.

And because you may beleeue me the better, I care not if I acquaint you with the circumstance.

I was informde of late dayes, that a certaine blind Retayler called the Diuell, vsed to lend money vpon pawnes, or any thing, / and [A2*v* would lette one for a neede haue a thousand poundes vppon a Statute Merchant of his soule: or if a man plide him thoroughly, would trust him vppon a Bill of his hande without any more circumstance. Besides, he was noted for a priuy Benefactor to Traitors and Parasites, and to aduance fooles and Asses far sooner than any, to be a greedy pursuer of newewes, and so famous a Politician in purchasing, that Hel (which at the beginning was but an obscure Village) is now become a huge Cittie, whereunto all Countries are tributary.

These manifest coniectures of Plentie, assembled in one common-place of abilitie; I determined to clawe Auarice by the elbowe, till his full belly gaue mee a full hande, and lette him bloud with my penne (if it might be) in the veyne of liberalitie: and so (in short time) was this Paper-monster *Pierce Penilesse* begotten.

But written and all, here lies the question; where shal I finde this olde Asse, that I may deliuer it? Masse thats true, they say the Lawyers haue the Diuell and all; and it is like enough he is playing Ambodexter amongst them. Fie, fie, the Diuell a driuer in Westminster hall, it can neuer be.

Now I pray what doe you imagine him to bee? Perhaps you thinke it is not possible he should bee so graue. Oh then you are in an errour, for hee is as formall as the best Scriuener of them all. Marry he doth not vse to weare a night-cap, for his hornes will not let him: and yet I know a hundred as well headed as he, that will make a iolly shift with a Court-cup on their crownes if the weather be colde.

To proceede with my tale, to Westminster hall I went, and made a search of Enquiry, from the blacke gown to the buckram bagge, if there were any such Sergeant, Bencher, Counsellor, Attorney, or Pettifogger, as *Signior Cornuto Diabolo*, with the good face. But they al (*vna voce*) affirmed, that he was not there: marry whether he were at the Exchaunge or no, amongst the rich Merchantes, that they could not tell: but it was likelier of the two, that I should meet with him, or heare of him at the least in those quarters. I faith, and say you so quoth I, and Ile bestowe a little labour more, but Ile hunt him out.

Without more circumstance, thither came I; and thrusting my / selfe, as the manner [A3 is, amongst the confusion of languages, I asked (as before) whether he were there extant or no? But from one to another, *Non noui Dæmonem* was all the answer I could get. At length (as Fortune serued) I lighted vpon an old stradling Vsurer, clad in a damaske cassocke edged with Fox fur, a paire of trunke slops, sagging down like a Shoomakers wallet, and a shorte thrid-bare gown on his backe, fac't with moatheaten budge, vpon his head he wore a filthy course biggin, and next it a garnish of night-caps, which a sage butten-cap, of the forme of a cow-sheard ouer spread very orderly: a fat chuffe it was I remember, with a gray beard cut short to the stumps, as though it were grimde, and a huge woorme-eaten nose, like a cluster of grapes hanging downe-wardes. Of him I demaunded if hee could tell my any tidings of the partie I sought for.

By my troth quoth he stripling, (and then he cought) I saw him not lately, nor know I certainely where he keepes: but thus much I heard by a Broker a friend of mine, that hath had some dealings with him in his time, that he is at home sicke of the gout and will not bee spoken withal, vnder more than thou art able to giue, some two or three hundred angels at least, if thou hast anie sute to him: & then parhapes hele straine curtesie with his legges in childe-bed, and come forth and talke with thee: but otherwise, *Non est domi*, hee is busie with *Mammon*, and the prince of the North, how to build vp his kingdome, or sending his spirites abroad to vndermine the maligners of his gouernment.

I hearing of this cold comfort, tooke me leaue of him verie faintly, and like a carelesse malecontent that knew not which way to turne, retired me to Paules to seeke my dinner with Duke *Humfrey*: but when I came there, the olde souldier was not vp: he is long a rising thought I, but thats all one: for he that hath no mony in his purse, must go dine with sir Iohn Best-betrust, at the signe of the chalk and the Post.

Two hungry turnes had I scarce fetcht in this wast gallery, when I was encountred by a neat pedantical fellow, in forme of a Cittizen: who thrusting himselfe abruptly into my companie like an Intelligencer, began very earnestly to question with me about the cause of my discontent, or what made me so sad, that seemed too yoong to be acquainted with sorrow. I nothing nice to vn- / fold my [A3v estate to any whatsoeuer, discourst to him the whole circumstaunce of my care: and what toyle and paines I had tooke in searching for him that would not be heard of. Why sir (quoth he) had I beene priuie to your purpose before, I could haue easd you of this trauell: for if it be the diuell you seeke for, know I am his man. I pray sir how might I call you? A knight of the Post quoth he, for so I am tearmed: a fellowe that will sweare you any thing for twelue pence, but indeed I am a spirite in nature and essence, that take vpon me this humaine shape, onely to set men together by the eares, and send soules by millions to hell.

Non bene conducti vendunt periuria testes.

Now trust me a substantiall trade, but

when doe you thinke you could send next to your maister? why euery day: for there is not a cormorant that dies, or Cut-purse that is hanged, but I dispatch letters by his soule to him, and to all my friends in the Low-cuntries: wherefore, if you haue any thing that you would haue transported: giue it me, and I will see it deliuered.

Yes marry haue I (quoth I) a certaine Supplication here vnto your Maister, which you may peruse if it please you. With that he opened it, and read as followeth. / [A4

To the high and mightie Prince of Darknesse, Donsell dell Lucifer, King of Acheron, Stixand Phlegeton, Duke of Tartary, marquesse of Conytus, and Lord high Regent of *Lymbo:* his distressed *Orator* Pierce Penilesse, *wisheth encrease of damnation,* and malediction eternall, Per Iesum Christum *Dominum nostrum.*

MOST humbly sueth vnto your sinfulnes, your singlesoald Orator *Pierce Penilesse*: that whereas your impious excellence, hath had the poore tennement of his purse any time this halfe yeer for your dauncing schoole, and he (notwithstanding) hath receiued no peny nor crosse for farme, according to the vsuall manner it may please your gracelesse Maiestie to consider of him, and giue order to your seruant Auarice, he may be dispatched, insomuch as no man heere in London can haue a dauncing schoole without rent, and his wit and knauerie cannot be maintained with nothing. Or if this be not so plausible to your honourable infernalship, it might seeme good to your helhood, to make extent vpon the soules of a number of vncharitable cormorants, who hauing incurd the daunger of a *Præmunire*, with medling with

No ile be sworne vppon a book haue I not.

casting foorth silken shraps to catch Woodcocks, or in syuing of Muckhils and shop-dust, whereof he will boult a whole cartload to gaine a bowd Pinne.

The description of dame Nigardize.

On the other side, Dame Niggardize his wife, in a sedge rug kirtle, that had beene a mat time out of minde, a course hempen raile about her shoulders, borrowed of the one end of a hop-bag, an apron made of Almanackes out of date (such as stand vpon Screens, or on the backside of a dore in a Chandlers shop), and an old wiues pudding pan on her head, thrumd with the parings of her nailes, sate barrelling vp the droppings of hir nose, in steed of oyle to saime wooll withall, and would not aduenture to spit without halfe a dozen porrengers at her elbow.

The house (or rather the hell) where these two Earthwormes / encaptiued this [B1 beautifull Substaunce, was vaste, large, strong buildt, and well furnished, all saue the Kitchin: for that was no bigger then the Cookes roome in a ship, with a little court chimney, about the compasse of a *Parenthesis* in proclamation print: then iudge you what diminutiue dishes came out of this doues-neast. So likewise of the Buttry, for whereas in houses of such stately foundation that are builte to outward shewe so magnificent, euery Office is answerable to the Hall, which is principall, there the Buttry was no more but a blind Cole-house vnder a paire of staires, wherein (vprising and downelying) was but one single single kilderkin of small beere, that would make a man with a carrouse of a spoonefull, runne through an Alphabet of faces. Nor vsd they any glasses or cups (as other men) but onely little farthing ounce boxes, whereof one of them fild vp with froath (in manner and forme of an Ale-house) was a meales allowance for the whole houshold. It were lamentable to tel what misery the Rattes and Mise endured in this hard world, how when all supply of vittualls failed them, they went a Boot-haling one night to Sinior Greedinesse bed-chamber, where finding nothing but emptines and vastitie, they encountred (after long inquisition) with a cod-peece, wel dunged and manured with greace (which my pinch-fart penie-father had retaind from his Bachelorship, vntill the eating of these presents). Vppon that they set, and with a couragious assault rent it cleene away from the breeches, and then carried it in triumph like a coffin on their shoulders betwixt them. The verie spiders and dust-weauers, that wont to set vp their loomes in euery window, decayed and vndone through the extreame dearth of the place, (that afforded them no matter to worke on) were constrained to breake against their wills, and goe dwell in the countrey, out of the reach of the broome and the wing: and generally, not a flea nor a cricket that caried any braue minde, that would stay there after he had once tasted the order of their fare. Onely vnfortunate gold (a predestinat slaue to drudges and fooles) liues in endlesse bondage ther amongst them, and may no way be releast, except you send the rot halfe a yeare amongst his keepers, and so make them away with a murrion one after another.

The complaint of pride.

O, but a far greater enormity raigneth in the hart of the Court: / Pride the peruerter [B1 v] of all Vertue, sitteth appareled in the Marchants spoiles, and ruine of yoong Citizens: and scorneth learning, that gaue their vpstart Fathers, titles of gentry.

The nature of an vpstart.

All malcontent sits the greasie son of a Cloathier, & complaines (like a decaied Earle) of the ruine of ancient houses: whereas the Weauers loomes first framed the web of his honor, & the lockes of wool that bushs and brambles haue tooke for toule of insolent sheep, that would needs striue for the wall of a fir bush, haue made him of the tenths of their tar, a Squier of low degree: and of the collectiõs of their scatterings, a Iustice *Tam Marti quam Mercurio*, of Peace & of Coram. Hee will bee humorous forsoth, and haue a broode of fashions by himselfe. Sometimes (because Loue commonly weares the liuerey of Wit) hee will be an *Inamorato Poeta*, & sonnet a whole quire of paper in praise of Lady *Swin-snout*, his yeolow fac'd Mistres, & weare a feather of her rainbeaten fan for a fauor, like a fore-horse. Al *Italionato* is his talke, & his spade peake is as sharpe as if he had been a Pioner before the walls of *Roan*. Hee will despise the barbarisme of his own Coũtrey, & tel a whole Legend of lyes of his trauailes vnto *Constantinople*. If he be challenged to fight, for his delatorye excuse hee obiects, that it is not the custome of the Spaniard or the Germaine to looke back to euery dog that barks. You shall see a dapper Iacke, that hath been but ouer at *Deepe*, wring his face round about, as a man would stir vp a mustard pot, & talke English through ye teeth like *Iaques Scabd-hams*, or *Monsieur Mingo de Moustrap*: when (poore slaue) he hath but dipt his bread in wilde Boares greace, and come home againe: or been bitten by the shins by a wolfe: and saith, he hath aduentured vpon the Barricadoes of *Gurney* or *Guingan*, and fought with the yong *Guise* hand to hand.

The counterfeit politian.

Some thinke to be counted rare Politicians and Statesmen, by being solitary: as who would say, I am a wise man, a braue man, *Secreta mea mihi: Frustra sapit, qui sibi non sapit*: and there no man worthy of my companie or friendship: when, although he goes vngartred like a malecontent Cutpursse, & weares his hat ouer his eies like one of the cursed crue, yet cãnot his stabing dagger, or his nittie loue lock keep him out of the legend of fantastical cockscombs. I pray ye good Moũsier diuel take some order, y[t] the / [B2 streetes be not pestered with them so as they are. Is it not a pitiful thing that a fellow that eates not a good meales meat in a weeke, but beggereth his belly quite and cleane, to make his backe a certaine kind of brokerly Gentleman: and nowe and then (once or twice in a Tearme) comes to the eighteene pence Ordenary, because hee would bee seen amongst Caualiers and braue courtiers, liuing otherwise all the yeere long with salt Butter and Holland cheese in his chamber, should take vppe a scornfull melancholy in his gate and countenance, and talke as though our common welth were but a mockery of gouernment, and our Maiestrates fooles, who wronged him in not looking into his deserts, not imploying him in State matters, and that if more regard were not had of him very shortly, the whole Realme should haue a misse of him, & he would go (I mary would he) where he should be more accounted of?

Is it not wonderfull ill prouided, I say, that this disdainfull companion is not made one of the fraternity of Fooles, to talke before great States, with some olde moth eaten Polititian, of mending high waies, and leading Armies into Fraunce?

The prodigall yoong Master.

A yoong Heyre or Cockney, that is his Mothers Darling, if hee haue playde the waste-good at the Innes of the Court or about London, and that neither his Students pension, nor his vnthrifts credite will serue to maintaine his Collidge of whores any longer, falles in a quarrelling humor with his fortune, because she made him not King of the *Indies*, and sweares and stares after ten in the hundreth, that nere a such Pesant as his Father or brother shall keepe him vnder, hee will to the sea and teare the gold out of the Spaniards throats but he will haue it, byrlady when he comes there, poore soule hee lyes in brine in Balist, and is lamentable sicke of the scuruies, his dainty fare is turned to a hungry feast of Dogs & Cats, or Haberdine and poore Iohn at the most, and which is lamentablest of all, that without Mustard.

As a mad Ruffion on a time, being in daunger of shipwrack by a tempest, and seeing all other at their vowes and praiers, that if it would please God of his infinite goodnesse, to delyuer them out of that imminent daunger, one woulde abiure this sinne wher vnto he was adicted: an other, make satisfaction for / that vyolence he had committed: [B2ᵛ he in a desperate iest, began thus to reconcile his soule to heauen.

O Lord, if it may seeme good to thee to deliuer me from this feare of vntimely death, I vowe before thy Throne and all thy starry Host, neuer to eate Haberdine more whilest I liue. Well, so it fell out that the Sky cleared, and the tempest ceased, and this carelesse wretch that made such a mockery of praier, readie to set foote a Land, cryed out: not without Mustard good Lord, not without Mustard: as though it had been the greatest torment in the world, to haue eaten Haberdine without Mustard. But this by the way, what pennance can be greater for Pride, than to let it swinge in his owne halter? *Dulce bellum in expertis*, theres no man loues the smooke of his owne Countrey, that hath not beene syngde in the flame of an other soyle. It is a pleasante thing ouer a full pot, to read the fable of thirsty *Tantalus:* but a harder matter to disgest salt meates at Sea, with stinking water.

An other misery of Pride it is, when men that haue good parts, and beare the name of deepe scholers: cannot be content to participate one faith with all Christendome, but because they will get a name to their vaineglory, they will set their selfe-loue to studie to inuent new sects of singularitie, thinking to liue when they are dead, by hauing sects called after their names, as *Donatists* of *Donatus Arrians* of *Arrius*: and a number more new faith-founders that haue made *England* the exchange of Innouations, and almost asmuch confusion of Religion in euery Quarter, as there was of tongues at the building of the Tower of *Babell*. Whence, a number that fetch the Articles of their Beleefe out of *Aristotle*, and thinke of heauen and hell as the Heathen Philosophers, take occasion to deride our Ecclesiasticall State, and all Ceremonies of Deuine worship, as bugbeares scar-crowes, because (like *Herodes* souldiers) we diuide Christs garment amongst vs in so many peeces, and of the vesture of saluation make some of vs Babies and apes coates, others straight trusses and Diuells breeches: some gally-gascoines or a shipmans hose like the Anabaptists and adulterous

The pride of the learned.

Familists, others with the Martinist a hood with two faces to hide their hypocrisie: & to conclude some like the Barrowists and Greenwodians, a garment full of the plague, which is not to be worne before it be new washt. / [B3

Hence Atheists triumph and reioyce, and talke as prophanely of the Bible, as of Beuis of Hampton. I heare say there be Mathematitions abroad, that will prooue men before *Adam*, and they are harboured in high places, who will maintaine it to the death, that there are no diuels.

The diuell hath children (as other men) but fewe of them know their owne father.

It is a shame (senior *Belzibub*) that you should suffer your selfe thus to be tearmed a bastard, or not approue to your predestinate children, not only that they haue a father, but that you are he that must owne them. These are but the suburbes of the sinne we haue in hand: I must describe to you a large cittie, wholy inhabited with this damnable enormitie.

The pride of Artificers.

In one place let me shew you a base Artificer, that hath no reuenues to boast on, but a Needle in his bosome; as braue as any Pensioner or Noble man.

The pride of Marchants wiues.

In an other corner, Mistris Minx a Marchants wife, that wil eate no Cherries forsooth, but when they are at twenty shillings a pound, that lookes as simperingly as if she were besmeard, and iets it as gingerly as if she were dancing the Canaries: she is so finicall in her speach, as though she spake nothing but what shee had first sewd ouer before in her Samplers, and the puling accent of her voyce is like a fained treble, or ones voyce that interprets to the puppets. What should I tel how squeamish she is in her dyet, what toyle she puts her poore seruaunts vnto, to make her looking glasses in the pauement? how she will not go into the field to cowre on the greene grasse, but she must haue a Coatch for her conuoy: and spends halfe a day in pranking her selfe if she be inuited to any strange place? Is not this the excesse of pride signior Sathan? Goe too, you are vnwise, if you make her not a chiefe Saint in your Calender.

The pride of pesants sprung vp of nothing.

The next obiect that encounters my eyes, is some such obscure vpstart gallants, as without desert or seruice are raised from the plough, to be checkmate with Princes: and these I can no better compare than to creatures that are bred *Sine coitu*, as crickets in chimnies, to which I resemble poore Scullians, that from turning spit in the chimney corner, are on the sodaine hoised vp from the Kitchin into the waiting chamber, or made Barons of the bieues, and Marquesses of the Marybones: some by corrupt water, as gnats, to which we may liken Brewers, that by retayling / filthy *Thames* water, come in [B3v] few yeares to bee worth fortie or fiftie thousand pound: others by dead wine, as little flying wormes, and so the Vintners in like case: others by slime as frogs, which may be alluded to Mother *Bunches* slimie ale, that hath made her, and some other of her fil-pot facultie so wealthie: others by dirt, as wormes, and so I know many gold-finers and hostlers come vp: some by hearbes, as cankers, and after the same sort our Apothecaries: others by ashes as *Scarabes*: and how else get our Colliers the pence? Others from the putrified flesh of dead beasts, as Bees of Buls, and Butchers by fli-blown beefe, waspes of horsses, and Hackney-men by selling their lame iades to hunts-men for carrion.

Sparagus a flowre that neuer groweth but throgh a mans dong.

Yet am I not against it, that these men by their mechanicall trades should come to be *Sparage* Gentlemen, and chuff-headed Burghomasters: but that better places should bee possessed by coystrels, and the Coblers crowe for crying but *Aue Cæsar*, bee more esteemed than rarer birds that haue warbled sweeter notes vnrewarded. But it is no meruaile: For as Hemlock fatteth Quailes, and Henbane Swine, which to all other is poyson: so some mens vices haue power to aduaunce them which would subuert any else that should seeke to climbe by them: and it is inough in them that they can pare their nailes well to get them a liuing, when as the seauen liberall Sciences and a good leg, will scarse get a scholler a paire of shoos, and a Canuas-dublet.

These whelpes of the first Litter of Gentilitie, these Exhalations, drawne vp to the heauen of honor, from the dunghill of abiect fortune, haue long been on horseback to come riding to your Diuelship: but I knowe not howe like Saint *George* they are alwaies mounted, but neuer moue. Here they outface Towne and countrey, and doo nothing but bandie factions with their betters. Theyr big limbes yeelde the Common-wealth no other seruice but idle sweate, and theyr heads like rough hewen Gloabes, are fit for nothing but to be the blockhouses of sleepe. *Raynold* the Fox may well beare vp his taile in the Lions denne, but when he comes abroad, hee is afraid of euery dogge that barkes. What Cur wil not bawle, and be ready to flie in a mans face, when he is set on by his maister, who if hee bee not by, to encourage him, he casts his taile betwixt his legs, & steales away like a sheepbyter. / *Vlisses* was a tall man [B4 vnder *Aiax* shield: but by himselfe hee would neuer aduenture but in the night. Pride is neuer built but vpon some pillers: and let his supporters faile him neuer so little, you shall finde him very humble in the dust. Wit oftentimes stands in stead of a chiefe arche to vnderproppe it, in souldiers strength, in women beautie.

The base insinuating of drudges and their practise to aspyre.

Drudges, that haue no extraordinarie gifts of body, nor of minde, filche themselues into some Noble mans seruice, either by bribes or by flattery, and when they are there, they so labour it with cap and knee, and plie it with priuie whisperings, that they wring themselues into his good opinion ere he be aware. Then do they vaunt themselues ouer the common multitude, and are readie to outbraue any man that stands by himselfe. Their Lords authoritie is as a rebater to beare vp the Peacocks taile of theyr boasting, and any thing that is said or doone to the vnhandsoming of their ambition, is straight wrested to the name of treson. Thus do weedes grow vp whiles no man regards them, and the Ship of Fooles is arriued in the Hauen of Felicitie, whilst the scoutes of Enuie contemne the attempts of any such small Barkes.

But beware you that be great mens

Fauorites: let not a seruile insinuating slaue creepe betwixt your legs into credit with your Lords: for pesants that come out of the colde of pouertie, once cherisht in the bosome of prosperitie, will straight forget that euer there was a winter of want, or who gaue them roome to warme them. The sonne of a churle cannot chuse but prooue ingratefull like his Father. Trust not a villaine that hath beene miserable, and is sodainly growne happie. Vertue ascendeth by degrees of desert vnto dignitie: golde and lust may lead a man a nearer way to promotion: but he that hath neither comlinesse nor coine to commend him, vndoubtedly strides ouer time by stratagems, *if of a mole-hil hee growes to a mountaine in a moment. This is that which I vrge, there is no friendship to be had with him, that is resolute to doe or suffer any thing, rather than to endure the destinie whereto he was borne: for he will not spare his owne Father or Brother, to make himselfe a Gentleman.

As by carrying tales or playing the doutie Pandor.

Fraunce, *Italy*, and *Spaine*, are all full of these false hearted *Machiuillions*: but properly Pride is the disease of the Spaniard, who is borne a Bragart in his mothers wombe: for if he be / but 17 yeeres old and hath [B4ᵛ come to the place where a Field was fought

The pride of the Spaniard.

(though halfe a yeare before) he then talks like one of the Giants that made warre against Heauen, and stands vppon his honour as much, as if hee were one of *Augustus* Souldiers, of whom he first instituted the order of Heralds: and let a man sooth him in his vaine of kilcow vanitie, you may commaund his heart out of his belly to make you a rasher on the coales, if you will next your heart.

The pride of the Italian.

The Italian is a more cunning proud fellowe, that hides his humour far cleanlier, and indeed seemes to take a pride in humilitie, and will profer a straunger more curtesie than hee meanes to performe. Hee hateth him deadly that takes him at his word: as for example, if vpon occasion of meeting, he request you to dinner or supper at his house, and that at the first or second intreatie you promise to bee his guest, he will be the mortalst enemie you haue: but if you deny him, he will thinke you haue manners and good bringing vp, and will loue you as his brother: marry at the third or fourth time you must not refuse him. Of all things he counteth it a mighty disgrace to haue a man passe iustling by him in hast on a narrowe causey, and aske him no leaue, which he neuer reuengeth with lesse then a stab.

The pride of the French man.

The Frenchman (not altered from his owne

nature) is wholly compact of deceiuable Courtship, and for the most part, loues none but himselfe and his pleasure: yet though he be the most *Grand Signeur* of them all, he will say, *A vostre seruice & commandemente Mounseur*, to the meanest vassaile he meets. Hee thinkes he doth a great fauour to that gentleman or follower of his, to whom he talks sitting on his close stoole: and with that fauour (I haue heard) the queene mother wonted to grace the Noble men of *France*: and a great man of their Nation comming in time past ouer into *England*, and beeing heere very honourably receiued, he in requital of his admirable entertainment, on an euening going to the priuie (as it were to honour extraordinaryly our english Lords, appointed to attend him) gaue one the candle, another his girdle, & another the paper: but they (not acquainted with this newe kinde of gracing) accompanying him to the priuy dore, set down the trash, & so left him: which he (considering what kindnes he extended to thẽ therin more than vsual) took hainously. /

The pride of the dane.

The most grosse and sencelesse proud [C1 dolts (in a different kind from all these) are the Danes: who stand so much vpon their vnweldy burliboand souldiery, that they account of no man that hath not a battle Axe

If you know him not by any of these marks look on hisfingers, & you shal be sure to find half a dozen siluer rings worth thre pence a peece.

at his girdle to hough dogs with, or weares not a cockes feather in a redde thrumd hat like a caualier: briefly, he is the best foole bragart vnder heauen. For besides, nature hath left him a flaberkin face, like one of the foure winds, and cheekes that sag like a womans dugs ouer his chin-bone, his apparel is so puft vp with bladders of Taffatie, and his back like biefe stuft with Parsly, so drawne out with Ribands and deuises, and blisterd with light sarcenet bastings, that you would thinke him nothing but a swarme of Butterflies, if you saw him a farre off.* Thus walkes he vp and downe in his Maiestie, taking a yard of ground at euery step, and stamps on the earth so terrible as if he ment to knocke vppe a spirite, when (foule drunken bezzle) if an Englishman set his little finger to him, he falles like a hogs-trough that is set on one end. Therfore I am the more vehement against them, because they are an arrogant Asse-headed people, that naturally hate learning, and all them that loue it: yea, and for they would vtterly roote it out from among them, they haue withdrawen al rewards from the Professors therof. Not *Barbary* it selfe is halfe so barbarous as they are. First, whereas the hope of honor maketh a Souldior in *England*: Byshopricks, Deanries, Prebendaries, and other priuate dignities, animate our Diuines to such excelence. The ciuil Lawyers haue their degrees & consistories of honour by themselues, equal in place with Knights and Esquiers: the common Lawyers, (suppose in the beginning they are but husband-mens sons) come in time to be chiefe Fathers of the land, and manie of them not the meanest of the Priuie Counsell.

No rewards amongst them for desert.

There the souldiour may fight himselfe out of his skinne, and do more exploites than he hath doytes in his purse, before from a common mercenary, he come to be Corporal of the mouldcheese: or the Lieutenant get a Captainship. None but the son of a Corporall must be a Corporall, nor any be Captaine, but the lawfull begotten of a Captaines body, Bishopricks, Deanries, Prebendaries, why they know no such functions: a sort of ragged Ministers they haue, of whom they count as basely, as water-bearers. / If any of their [C1v Noblemen refraine three howers in his life time from drinking, to study the Lawes, hee may perhaps haue a little more gouernment put into his hands than another: but otherwise, Burgomasters and Gentlemen beare all the swaye of both swords, spirituall and temporall. It is death there for anie but a husbandman to marry a husbandmans daughter, or a Gentlemans childe to ioyne with any but the sonne of a Gentleman, marry this the King may well banish, but hee cannot put a Gentleman vnto death in any cause whatsoeuer, which makes them stand vppon it so proudly as they doe. For fashion sake some will put their children to schoole, but they set them not to it till they are foureteene yeere olde: so that you shall see a great boy with a beard learne his A B C. and sit weeping vnder the rod, when he is thirtie yeeres old.

What it is to make men labor without hope.

I will not stande to inferre, what a preiudice it is to the thrift of a florishing State, to poyson the growth of glory, by giuing it nought but the puddle water of penury to drinke: to clippe the winges of a high towring Faulcon, who, wheras she wont in her feathered youthfulnesse, to looke with an amiable eye vppon her gray breast, and her speckled side sayles, all sinnowed with siluer quilles, and to dryue whole Armies of fearefull fowle before her to her maisters Table: now she sits sadly on the ground, picking of wormes, mourning the crueltie of those vngentleman-like idle hands, that dismembred the beauty of her trayne.

You all knowe, that man (insomuch as hee is the Image of God) delighteth in honour and worship, and all holy Writ warrantes that delight, so it bee not derogatory to any part of Gods owne worship: now take away that delight, a discontented idlenesse ouertakes him. For his hire, any handycraft man, be he Carpenter, Ioyner, or Painter, wil ploddingly do his day labor: but to adde credit and fame to his workmanship, or to winne a maistery to himselfe aboue all other, hee will make a further assay in his trade, than euer hitherto he did, hee will haue a thousand florishes which before he neuer thought vpon, and in one day ridde more out of hand, than earst hee did in ten: So in Armes, so in Artes, if titles of fame and glory be proposed to forward minds, or that soueraigntie (whose sweetnes they haue not yet felt) be set in likely view for them to sore too, they will make a ladder of cord of the / links of their [C2 braines, but they will fasten their handes as well as their eies, on the imaginatiue blisse, which they already enioy by admiration. Experience reproues me for a foole, for dilating on so manifest a case.

The Danes are bursten-bellied sots, that are to bee confuted with nothing but Tankards or quart pots, and *Ouid* might as well haue read his verses to the *Getes* that vnderstood him not, as a man talk reason to them that haue no eares but their mouths nor sense but of that which they swallowe downe their throates. God so loue me, as I loue the quicke-witted Italians, and therefore loue them the more, because they mortally detest this surley swinish Generation.

I need not fetch colours from other countries to paint the vglie visage of Pride, since her picture is set forth in so many painted faces here at home. What drugs, what sorceries, what oiles, what waters, what oyntments, doe our curious Dames vse to inlarge their withered beauties? Their lips are as lauishly red, as if they vsed to kisse an okerman euery morning, and their cheeks sugercandied and cherry blusht so sweetly, after the colour of a newe Lord Mayors postes, as if the pageant of their wedlocke holiday were harde at the doore; so that if a Painter were to drawe any of their Counterfets on Table, he needes no more but wet his pencill, and dab it on their cheekes, and he shall haue vermillion and white enough to furnish out his worke, though he leaue his tar-boxe at home behind him. Wise was that sin-washing Poet that made the Ballet of Blue starch and poaking stickes, for indeed the lawne of licentiousnesse hath consumed all the wheat of hospitalitie. It is said Laurence Lucifer, that you went vp and downe London crying then like a lanterne & candle man. I meruaile no

Laundresse would giue you the washing and starching of your face for your labour, for God knowes it is as black as the blacke Prince.

It is suspected you haue beene a great *Tobacco* taker in your youth, which causeth it to come so to passe: but Dame Nature your nurse was partly in fault, else she might haue remedied it. She should haue noynted your face ouernight with *Lac virginis*, which baking vpon it in bed till the morning, she might haue pild off the scale like the skin of a custard, and making a pos- / set of vergis [C2v mixt with the oyle of Tartary and Camphire, bathde it in it a quarter of an houre, and you had been as faire as the floure of the frying pan. I warrant we haue old hacksters in this great Grandmother of Corporations, Madame *Troynouant*, that haue not backbited any of their neighbours with the tooth of enuy this twentie yeare, in the wrinckles of whose face, ye may hide false dice, and play at cherry-pit in the dint of their cheekes, yet these aged mothers of iniquitie will haue their deformities newe plaistred ouer, and weare nosegayes of yeolow haire on their furies foreheads, when age hath written Hoe God be here, on their bald burnt parchment pates. Pish, pish, what talke you of old age or balde pates? men and women that haue gone vnder the South pole, must lay off their furde night-caps in spight of their teeth, and become yeomen of the Vineger bottle: a close periwig hides all the sinnes of an olde whore-master, but *Cucullus non facit Monachum:* tis not their newe bonnets will keepe them from the old boanach. Ware when a mans sins are written on his ey-browes, and that there is not a haire bredth betwixt them and the falling sicknes. The times are daungerous: and this is an yron age, or rather no yron age, for swordes and bucklers goe to pawne a pace in Long-Lane: but a tinne age; for tinne and pewter are more esteemed than Latine. You that bee wise despise it, abhorre it, neglect it; for what shoulde a man care for gold that cannot get it.

The commendation of Antiquaries. Laudamus veteres, sed nostris vtimur annis.

An Antiquarie is an honest man, for hee had rather scrape a peece of copper out of the durt, than a crowne out of *Ploydens* standish. I know many wise Gentlemen of this mustie vocation, who out of loue with the times wherein they liue, fall a retayling of *Alexanders* stirrops, because (in veritie) there is not suche a strong peece of stretching leather made now adayes, nor yron so well tempred for any money. They will blow their nose in a boxe, & say it is the spettle that *Diogenes* spet in ones face: who being inuited to dinner to his house, that was neat & braue in all points as might be deuised; and the grunting Dogge somewhat troubled with the rheume (by meanes of his long fasting and staying for dinner more than wont) spet full in his Hostesse face: and beeing askt the reason of it, said; it was the foulest place he could spie out in all his house. Let their Mistresse (or some other woman) / giue them a feather [C3 of her fanne for her fauour, and if one aske them what it is? they make answer, a plume of the Phenix, wherof there is but one in all the whole world. A thousand guegawes and toyes haue they in their chambers, which they heape vp together with infinite expence, and are made beleeue of them that sell them, that they are rare and pretious thinges, when they haue gathered them vpon some dunghill, or rakte them out of the kennell by chance. I know one sold an old rope with foure knots on it for foure pound, in that he gaue it out, it was the length and breadth of Christs Tombe. Let a Tinker take a peece of brasse worth a halfe penie, and set strange stamps on it, and I warrant he may make it more worth to him of some fantasticall foole, than all the kettels that euer he mended in his life. This is the disease of our newfangled humorists, that know not what to doe with their welth.

It argueth a very rusty witte, so to doate on worme-eaten Elde.

The complaint of Enuie.

OVT vpon it, how long is Pride a dressing her selfe? Enuie awake for thou must appear before *Nicalao Maleuolo* great Muster maister of hell. Marke you this slie mate, how smoothly hee lookes? The Poets were ill aduised, that fained him to be a leane gag toothd Beldam with hollow eyes, pale cheeks, and snakie heire: for he is not onely a man, but a iolly lusty old Gentleman, that will winke, and laugh, and ieast drily, as if he were the honestest of a thousand: and I warrant you shall not heare a foule word come from him in a yeare. I wil not contradict it, but the Dog may worry a sheepe in the dark, & thrust his necke into the collar of clemency & pity when he hath don: as who shold say, God forgiue him, hee was a sleepe in the shambles, when the innocent was done to death. But openly, Enuie sets a ciuil fatherly countenance vpon it, & hath not so much as a drop of bloud in his face to attaint him of murther. I thought it expedient in this my Supplication, to place it next to Pride: for it is his adopted sonne. And hence comes it, that proud men repine at others prosperitie, and greeue that any should be great but themselues. *Mens cuiusque, is est quisque:* it is a

Prouerbe that is as hoary as Dutch-butter. If a man wil go to the diuell, he may go to the diuell: there are a thousand iugling tricks to be vsed at hey passe come aloft: & the world hath cords enough to trus vp a calf that stands in ons way. / Enuie is a Crocodile that [C3v weepes when he kils, and fights with none but he feedes on. This is the nature of this quick-sighted monster, he will endure any paynes to endamage another, waste his body with vnder-taking exploytes that would require tenne mens strengths, rather than any should get a penny but himselfe, bleare his eyes to stand in his neighbours light; and to conclude, like *Atlas* vnder-proppe heauen alone, rather than any should be in heauen that hee likte not of, or come vnto heauen by any other meanes but by him.

You goodman wandrer about the world, how doe yee spende your time, that you do not rid vs of these pestilent members? you are vnworthy to haue an office if you can execute it no better. Behold another enemy of mankinde besides thy selfe exalted in the South, *Philip* of Spaine, who not content to bee the God of gold, and chiefest commaunder of content that Europe affoords, but now he doth nothing but thirst after humane bloud, when his foot is on the thresholde of the

Philip of Spaine, as great an enemy to mankind as the diuell.

graue: and as a Wolfe beeing about to deuoure a horse, doth balist his belly with earth, that hee may hang the heauier vppon him, and then forcibly flyes in his face, neuer leauing his hold till he hath eaten him vp: so this woluish vnnaturall vsurper, being about to deuoure all Christendom by inuasion, doth cram his treasures with Indian earth, to make his malice more forcible, and then flyes in the bosome of *Fraunce* and *Belgia*, neuer withdrawing his forces (as the Wolfe his fastning) till he hath deuoured their welfare, & made the war-wasted carcases of both kingdomes a pray for his tyranny. Onely poore *England* giues him bread for his cake, and holdes him out at the armes end. His Armadoes (y[t] like a high wood ouer-shadowed the shrubs of our low ships) fled from the breath of our Cannons, as vapors before the Sun, or as the Elephant flies from the Ram, or the Sea Whale from the noyse of parched bones. The winds enuying that the aire should be dimmed with such a *Chaos* of wodden clouds, raised vp high bulwarks of bellowing waues, whence Death shot at their disordred Nauy: and the Rockes with their ouer-hanging iawes, eate vp all the fragments of oake that they left. So perisht our foes, so the Heauens did fight for vs. *Præterit Hippomenes, resonant spectacula plausu.*

I do not doubt (Doctor Diuell) but you were present in this / action or passion [C4 rather, and helpt to bore holes in ships, to make them sinke faster; and rence out Galley-foistes with salt water, that stunke like fustie barrels with their Maisters feare. It will be a good while ere you doe as much for the King, as you did for his subiects. I would haue ye perswade an Armie of goutie Vsurers to go to Sea vppon a boon voyage: trie if you can tempt Enuy to embarke himself in the mal'aduenture, and leaue troubling the streame, that Poets and good fellowes may drinke, and Souldiers may sing *Placebo*, that haue murmured so long at the waters of strife.

But that wil neuer be: for so long as Pride, Riot, and whoredome are the companions of yoong Courtiers, they wil alwayes bee hungry, and ready to bite at euery Dog that hath a boane giuen him beside themselues. Iesu, what secret grudge and rancor raignes amongst them, one being ready to dispaire of himself, if he see the Prince but giue his fellow a faire looke: or to die for griefe if he be put down in brauery neuer so little. Yet this custome haue our false harts fetcht from other countries, that they will sweare and protest loue, where they hate deadly, and smile on him most kindly, whose subuersion in soule they haue vowed. *Fraus sublimi regnat in aula.* Tis rare to finde a true frend in Kings Pallaces; Either thou must be so miserable, that thou fall into the hands of scornful pitie, or thou canst not escape the sting of enuy. In one thought assemble the famous men of all ages, and tel me which of them all sate in the sun-shine of his soueraignes grace, or wext great of low beginnings, but he was spite-blasted, heaued at, & ill spoken of: and that of those that bare them most countenaunce. But were enuy nought but wordes, it might seeme to bee onely womens sinne: but it hath a lewde mate hanging on his sleeue, called Murther, a sterne fellowe, that (like a Spanyard in fight) aymeth all at the heart: hee hath more shapes than *Proteus*, and will shifte himselfe vppon any occasion of reuengement, into a mans dish, his drinke, his apparell, his ringes, his stirrops, his nosegay.

Murder, the companion of Enuie.

O Italy,* the Academic of man-slaughter, the sporting place of murther, the Apothecary shop of poyson for all Nations: how many kind of weapons hast thou inuented for malice? Suppose I loue a mans wife whose husband yet liues, and cannot enioy / her [C4v] for his iealous ouer-looking: Physicke, or rather the art of murther (as it may be vsed) will lend one a Medicine which shall make

Italie, the storehouse of all murderous inuentions.

him away, in the nature of that disease he is most subiect to, whether in the space of a yeare, a moneth, halfe a yeare, or what tract of time you will, more or lesse.

In Rome the Papal Chayre is washt euery fiue yeare at the furthest with this oyle of Aconitum. I pray God the King of Spayne feasted not our holy father *Sextus*, that was last, with such conserue of Henbane, for it was credibly reported hee loued him not, & this that is now, is a God made with his owne hands as it may appeare by the *Pasquil* that was set vp of him, in manner of a note, presently after his election. *Sol*, *Re*, *Me*, *Fa*. that is to say: *Solus Rex me facit*; onely the K. of Spaine made me Pope. I am no Chronicler from our owne Countrey, but if probable suspition might bee heard vppon his oath, I thinke some mens soules would not bee canonized for Martyrs, that on the earth did sway it as Monarches.

The Pasquil that was made vpon this last Pope.

As Cardinal Wholsey for example.

Is it your will and pleasure (noble *Lantsgraue* of *Lymbo*) to let vs haue lesse carousing to your health in poison, fewer vnder hand conspirings, or open quarrels, executed onely in wordes, as they are in the world now a dayes: & if men wil needs carouse, conspire, and quarrell, that they may make Ruffians hall of Hell: and there, bandy balles of

Brimstone at one anothers head, and not trouble our peaceable Paradise with their priuate hurliburlies about strumpets, where no weapon (as in *Adams* Paradise) should bee named: but onely the Angell of prouidence stand with a fiery sword at the gate, to keep out our enemies.

The complaint of Wrath, a branch of Enuie.

A Perturbation of mind (like vnto Enuy) is Wrath, which looketh farre lower than the former: For whereas Enuie cannot be saide to bee, but in respect of our Superiours, Wrath respecteth no degrees nor persons, but is equally armed agaynst all that offende him. A hare-braind little Dwarfe it is, with a swarth visage, that hath his hart at his tongues end, if he be contraride, and will be sure to do no right nor take no wrong. If hee bee a Iudge or a Iustice, (as some-times the Lyon comes to giue sentence against the Lamb) then he sweares by nothing but by Saint Tyborne, & makes Newgate a Nowne Substantiue, / whereto all his other words [D1 are but Adiectiues. Lightly hee is an olde man: (for those yeares are most wayward and teatish) yet be he neuer so old or so froward, since Auarice like-wise is a fellow vice of those fraile yeares, wee must set one extreame to striue with another, and alay the anger of

Littlemen for the most part are most angry.

New gate, a common name for al prisons, as Homo is a common name for a man or a woman.

oppression, by the sweet incense of a newe purse of angels: or the doting Planet may haue such predominance in these wicked Elders of *Israel*, that if you send your wife or some other female to plead for you, shee may get your pardon vpon promise of better acquaintance. But whist, these are the workes of darknesse and may not be talkt of in the day time: Fury is a heate or fire, & must bee quencht with maides water.

Amongst other cholericke wise Iustices, he was one, that hauing a play presented before him and his Towne-ship, by *Tarlton* and the rest of his fellowes her Maiesties seruants, and they were now entring into their first merriment (as they call it) the people began exceedingly to laugh, when *Tarlton* first peept out his head. Whereat the Iustice not a little moued, and seeing with his beckes and nods hee could not make them cease, he went with his staffe, and beat them round about vnmercifully on the bare pates, in that they being but Farmers & poore countrey Hyndes would presume to laugh at the Queenes men, and make no more account of her cloath in his presence.

A tale of a wise Iustice.

The causes conducting vnto wrath are as diuers, as the actions of a mans life. Some will take on like a mad man, if they see a pigge

The nature of the Irish man

come to the table. *Sotericus* the Surgeon was cholericke at the sight of Sturgeon. The Irishman will drawe his dagger, and bee ready to kill and slay, if one breake winde in his company: and so some of our English men that are Souldiers, if one giue them the lye: but these are light matters, whereof *Pierce* complaineth not.

Be aduertised Master *Os fœtidum*, Bedle of the Blackesmithes, that Lawyers cannot deuise which way in the world to begge, they are so troubled with brabblements and sutes euery Tearme, of Yeomen and Gentlemen that fall out for nothing.

If *Iohn a Nokes* his henne doo but leap into *Elizabeth de Gappes* close, shee will neuer leaue to haunt her husband, till he bring it to a *Nisi prius*. One while, the Parson sueth the / parishioner for bringing home [D1v] his tythes: another while, the Parishioner sueth the Parson for not takinge away his Tythes in time.

A merry tale of a Butcher & his Calues.

I heard a tale of a Butcher, who driuing two Calues ouer a Com-mon, that were coupled together by the neckes with an Oken With, in the way wher they shold passe, there lay a poore leane Mare with a galde backe, to whome they comming (as chance fell out) one of one side, and the other of the other, smelling on her (as their manner is) the midst of the With that was betwixt their necks, rubd her and grated her on the sore backe, that shee started and rose vp, and hung them both on her backe as a beame, which being but a rough plaister to her raw vlcer, shee ran away with them (as she were fran-tick) into the Fens, where the Butcher could not follow them, and drownde both her selfe and them in a Quagmyre. Now the owner of the Mare is in lawe with the Butcher for the losse of his Mare, and the Butcher enterchangably endites him for his Calues. I pray ye Timothy Tempter, bee an Arbitrator bee twixt them, and couple them both by the neckes (as the Calues were) and carry them to Hel on your backe, and then I hope they wyll be quiet.

The chiefe spur vnto wrath is Drunkennes, which as the touch of an Ashenbough, causeth a gidinesse in the Vipers head, and the Batte lightly strooke with the leafe of a Tree, loseth his remembrance: so they being but lightly sprinckled with the iuyce of the Hop, become sencelesse, and haue their reason strooken blind, as soone as euer the Cup scaleth the Fortresse of their Nose. Then run their words at random like a dog that hath lost his master, and are vppe with this man and that man, and generally inuay against al men: but those that keep a wet corner for a friend, and will not thinke scorne to drinke with a good fellowe and a Souldiour: and so long do they practise this vaine on their Ale-bench, that when they are sober they cannot leaue it. There be those that get their liuing al the yeere long, by nothing but rayling.

A tale of one Fryer Charles, a foule mouthde knaue.

Not Farre from *Chester*, I knewe an odde foule mouthde knaue, called *Charles* the Fryer, that had a face so parboyled with mens spitting on it, and a backe so often knighted in Bridewell, that it was impossible for any shame or punishment, to terri- / fie him [D2 from ill speaking, Noblemen he would liken to more vgly things than himself: some to After my hartie commendations, with a dash ouer the head: others, to guilded chines of beefe, or a shoomaker sweating, when he puls on a shoo: another to an old verse in *Cato*, *Ad consilium ne accesseris antequam voceris:* another, to a Spanish Codpisse: another, that his face was not yet finisht, with such like innumerable absurd illusions: yea, what was he in the Court, but he had a comparison in stead of a Capcase to put him in. Vpon a time being chalenged at his owne weapon in a priuate Chamber, by a great personage, (rayling I meane) he so far outstript him in vilanious words, and ouerbandied him in bitter tearmes, that the name of sport could not perswade him patience, nor containe his furie in any degrees of ieast, but needs hee must wreake himselfe vppon him: neither would a common reuenge suffice him, his displeasure was so infinite (and it may be common reuenges he tooke before, as far as the whipcord would stretch, vpon like prouokements) wherefore he caused his men to take him, and brickt him vp in a narrow chimney, that was *Neque maior neque minor corpore locato*, where he fed him for fifteene dayes with bread and water through a hole, letting him sleep standing if he would, for lye or sit he could not, and then he let him out to see if he could learne to rule his tongue any better.

It is a disparagement to those that haue any true sparke of Gentilitie, to be noted of the whole world so to delight in detracting, that they should keepe a venemous toothd Cur, and feed him with the crums that fall from their table, to do nothing but bite euery one by the shins that passe by. If they will needes be merry, let them haue a foole and not a knaue to disport them, and seeke some other to bestow their almes on, than such an impudent begger.

As there be those that rayle at all men, so there be those that raile at all Arts, as

Cornelius Agrippa De vanitate scientiarum, and a Treatise that I haue seene in dispraise of learning, where he saith, it is the corrupter of the simple, the schoolemaister of sin, the storehouse of treacherie, the reuiuer of vices, and mother of cowardize, alledging many examples, how there was neuer man egregiously euill, but he was a Scholler: that when the / vse of letters was first inuented, the [D2v Golden World ceased, *Facinusque inuasit mortales:* how studie dooth effeminate a man, dim his sight, weaken his braine, and ingender a thousand diseases. Small learning would serue to confute so manifest a scandale, and I imagine all men like my selfe so vnmoueablie resolued of the excellencie thereof, that I will not by the vnderpropping of confutation seeme to giue the idle witted aduersarye so much encouragement, as hee should surmize his superficiall arguments had shaken the foundation of it: against which hee could neuer haue lifted his penne, if her selfe had not helpt him to hurte her selfe.

An inuectiue against enemies of Poetrie.

Absit arrogantia, that this speeche shold concerne all diuines, but such dunces as

With the enemies of Poetrie, I care not if I haue a bout, and those are they that tearme our best Writers but babling Ballat-makers, holding them fantasticall fooles, that haue wit, but cannot tell how to vse it, I my selfe haue beene so censured among some dul-headed

*Diuines: who deeme it no more cunning to wryte an exquisite Poem, than to preach pure *Caluin*, or distill the iustice of a Commentary in a quarter Sermon. Prooue it when you will, you slowe spirited Saturnists, that haue nothing but the pilfries of your penne, to pollish an exhortation withall: no eloquence but Tautologies, to tie the eares of your Auditorye vnto you: no inuention but heere is to bee noted, I stoale this note out of *Beža* or *Marlorat*: no wit to mooue, no passion to vrge, but onelye an ordinarie forme of preaching, blowne vp by vse of often hearing and speaking: and you shall finde there goes more exquisite paines and puritie of witte, to the writing of one such rare Poem as *Rosamond*, than to a hundred of your dunsticall *Sermons.

abridge men of their lawfull liberty and care not howe vnprepared they speake to their Auditorie.

Such Sermons I meane as our sectuaries preach in ditches and other Conuenticles when they leape from the Coblers stal to their pulpits.

Should we (as you) borrowe all out of others, and gather nothing of our selues, our names should bee baffuld on euerie Bookesellers Stall, and not a Chandlers Mustard-pot but would wipe his mouthe with our wast paper. Newe Herrings, new, wee must crye, euery time wee make our selues publique, or else we shall bee christened with a hundred newe tytles of Idiotisme. Nor is Poetrie an Arte, whereof there is no vse in a mans whole lyfe, but to describe discontented thoughts and youthfull desires: for there is no studie, but it dooth illustrate and beautifie. How admirablie shine those Di- / uines aboue [D3 the common mediocritie, that haue tasted the sweete springs of *Pernassus*?

Encomium H. Smithi.

Siluer tongu'd *Smith* whose well tun'd stile hath made thy death the generall teares of the Muses, queintlie couldst thou deuise heauenly Ditties to *Apolloes* Lute, and teach stately verse to trip it as smoothly, as if *Ouid* and thou had but one soule. Hence alone did it proceed, that thou wert such a plausible pulpit man that before thou entredst into the rough waies of Theologie, thou refinedst, preparedst, and purifidest thy minde with sweete Poetrie. If a simple mans censure may be admitted to speake in such an open Theater of opinions, I neuer saw aboundant reading better mixt with delight, or sentences which no man can challenge of prophane affectation, sounding more melodious to the eare or piercing more deepe to the heart.

The fruits of Poetry.

To them that demaund what fruites the Poets of our time bring forth, or wherein they are able to proue themselues necessary to the state. Thus I answere. First and for most, they haue cleansed our language from barbarisme and made the vulgar sort here in *London* (which is the fountaine whose riuers flowe round about *England*) to aspire to a richer puritie of speach, than is communicated with the Comminaltie of any Nation vnder heauen. The vertuous by their praises they encourage to be more vertuous, to vicious men they are as infernall hags to haunt their ghosts with eternall infamie after death. The Souldier in hope to haue his high deeds celebrated by their pens, despiseth a whole Armie of perills, and acteth wonders exceeding all humane coniecture. Those that care neither for God nor the diuell, by their quills are keept in awe. *Multi famam* (saith one) *pauci conscientiam verentur*.

Let God see what he will, they would be loath to haue the shame of the world. What age will not praise immortal *Sir Phillip Sidney*, whom noble *Salustius* (that thrice siguler french Poet) hath famoused: together with *Sir Nicholas Bacon* Lord keeper, & merry sir *Thomas Moore*, for the chiefe pillers of our english speech. Not so much but *Chaucers* host, *Baly* in Southworke, & his wife of Bath he keeps such a stirre with, in his *Canterbury* tales, shalbe talkt of whilst the Bath is vsde, or there be euer a bad house in Southwork. Gentles, it is not your lay Chro- / ni- [D3v graphers, that write of nothing but of Mayors and Sheriefs and the deare yeere, and the

Plin.lib.3.

The dispraise of laie chronigraphers.

great Frost, that can endowe your names with neuer dated glory: for they want the wings of choise words to fly to heauen, which we haue: they cannot sweeten a discourse, or wrest admiration from men reading, as we can: reporting the meanest accident. Poetry is the hunny of all flowers, the quintessence of all Sciences, the Marrowe of Witte, and the very Phrase of Angels: how much better is it then to haue an eligant Lawier to plead ones cause, than a stutting Townsman that loseth himselfe in his tale, and doth nothing but make legs: so much it is better for a Nobleman or Gentleman, to haue his honours story related, and his deedes emblazond by a Poet, than a Citizen.

Alas poore latinlesse Authors, they are so simple they know not what they doe; They no sooner spy a new Ballad, and his name to it that compilde it: but they put him in for one of the learned men of our time, I maruell how the Masterlesse men, that set vp their bills in Paules for seruices, & such as paste vp their papers on euery post, for Arithmetique and writing Schooles, scape eternity amongst them; I beleeue both they and the Knight Marshals men, that naile vp *Mandates* at the Court gat, for annoying the Pallace with filth or making water, if they set their names to the writing, will shortly make vp the number of the learned men of our time, and be as famous as the rest. For my part I do challenge no praise of learning to my selfe, yet haue I worne a gowne in the Vniuersitie, and so hath *caret tempus non habet moribus:* but this I dare presume that if any *Mecœnas* binde me to him by his bounty or extend some sound liberalitie to mee worth the speaking of, I will doo him as much honour as any Poet of my beardlesse yeeres shall in *England.* Not that I am so confident what I can doe, but that I attribute so much to my thankfull minde aboue others, which I am perswaded would enable me to worke myracles.

On the contrary side, if I bee euill intreated, or sent away with a Flea in mine eare, let him looke that I will raile on him soundly: not for an houre or a day, whiles the iniury is fresh in my memory: but in some elaborate pollished Poem, which I will leaue to the world when I am dead, to be a liuing Image / to all ages, [D4 of his beggerly parsimony and ignoble illiberaltie: and let him not (whatsoeuer he be) measure the weight of my words by this booke, where I write *Quic quid in buccam venerit*, as fast as my hand can trot: but I haue tearmes (if I be vext) laid in sleepe in *Aquafortis*, & Gunpowder, that shall rattle through

I wold tell you in whatbook it is, but I am afraid it would make his booke sell in his latter daies, which hetherto hath lien dead and beene a greatlosse to the Printer.

the Skyes and make an Earthquake in a Pesants eares. Put case (since I am not yet out of the Theame of Wrath) that some tired Iade belonging to the Presse, whom I neuer wronged in my life; hath named me expressely in Print (as I will not do him) and accuse me of want of learning, vpbraiding me for reuiuing in an epistle of mine the reuerent memory of Sir *Thomas Moore*, Sir *Iohn Cheeke*, Doctor *Watson*, Doctor *Haddon*, Doctor *Carre*, Maister *Ascham*, as if they were no meate but for his Maisterships mouth, or none but some such as the son of a ropemaker were worthy to mention them. To shewe how I can raile, thus would I begin to raile on him. Thou that hadst thy hood turnd ouer thy eares when thou wert a Batchelor, for abusing of *Aristotle*, & setting him vpon the Schoole gates painted with Asses eares on his head: is it any discredit for me, thou great *babound*, thou *Pigmie Braggart*, thou Pamphleter of nothing but **Peants*, to bee censured by thee, that hast scorned the Prince of Philosophers; thou that in thy Dialogues soldst Huny for a halpeny, and the choycest Writers exant for cues a peece, that camest to the Logicke Schooles when thou wert a Fresh-man and writst phrases, off with thy gowne and vntrusse, for I meane to lash thee mightily.

Looke at the Chandlers shop, or at the Flaxwiues stall, if you see no tow nor Sope

Thou hast a Brother hast thou not, student in Almanackes, go too, Ile stand to it, fatherd one of thy bastards (a booke I meane) which being of thy begetting was set forth vnder his name.

wrapt vp in the title page of such a Pamphlet, as Incerti Authoris Io pæan.

Gentlemen, I am sure you haue hearde of a ridiculous Asse that many yeares since sold lyes by the great, and wrote an absurd *Astrologicall Discourse* of the terrible Coniunction of *Saturne* and *Iupiter*, wherein (as if hee had lately cast the Heauens water, or beene at the anatomizing of the Skies intrailes in Surgeons hall) hee prophecieth of such strange wonders to ensue from stars destemperature, and the vnuseall adultrie of Planets, as none but he that is Bawd to those celestiall bodies, could euer discry. What expectation there was of it both in townc / and country, the [D4v] amazement of those times may testifie: and the rather because he pawned his *credit vpon it, in these expresse tearmes; *If these things fall not out in euery point as I haue wrote, let me for euer hereafter loose the credit of my Astronimie*. Well so it happened, that he happened not to be a man of his word; his Astronimie broke his day with his creditors and *Saturne* and *Iupiter* prou'd honester men then all the World tooke them for: whereupon, the poore Prognosticator was ready to runne himselfe

Which at home i wis, was worth a dozen of halters at least, for if I be not deceiued, his father was a Rope-maker.

through with his *Iacobs* Staffe, and cast himselfe headlong from the top of a Globe (as a mountaine) and breake his necke. The whole Vniuersitie hyst at him, *Tarlton* at the Theator made iests of him, and *Elderton* consumd his ale-crummed nose to nothing, in bearbayting him with whole bundles of ballets. Would you in likely reason gesse it were possible for any shame-swolne toad to haue the spet-proofe face to out liue this disgrace? It is deare brethren, *Viuit imo viuit*, and which is more, he is a Vicar.

Poor Slaue, I pitie thee that thou hadst no more grace but to come in my way. Why, could not you haue sate quiet at home, and write Catechismes, but you must be comparing me to *Martin*? and exclayme against me for reckoning vp the high Schollers of worthy memory? *Iupiter ingeniis prabat sua numina vatum*, saith *Ouid*: *Seque celebrari quolibet ore sinit*. Which if it be so, I hope I am *Aliquis*, and those men *quos honoris causa nominaui*, are not greater than gods. Me thinks I see thee stand quiuering and quaking, and euen now lift vp thy hands to heauen, as thanking God my choler is somewhat asswag'd: but thou art deceiued, for how euer I let fall my stile a little to talke in reason with thee that hast none, I do not meane to let thee scape so.

Thou hast wronged one for my sake (whom for the name I must loue) *T. N.* the Maister Butler of Pembrooke Hall, a farre better Scholler than thy selfe (in my iudgement) and one that sheweth more discretion and gouernment, in setting vp a sise of Bread, than thou in all thy whole booke. Why man, thinke no scorne of him for he hath held thee vp a hundred times, whiles the Deane hath giuen thee correction, and thou hast capt and kneed him (when thou wert hungrie) for a chipping. But thats nothing, for hadst thou neuer beene beholding to him, nor holden / vp by him, [E1 he hath a Beard that is a better Gentleman than all thy whole body, and a graue countenance like *Cato*, able to make thee run out of thy wits for feare, if he looke sternly vpon thee. I haue reade ouer thy Sheepish discourse of the Lambe of GOD and his enemies, and entreated my patience to be good to thee whilst I reade: but for all that I could doe with my selfe, (as I am sure I may doe as much as another man) I could not refraine, but bequeath it to the Priuie, leafe by leafe as I read it, it was so vgly, dorbellicall and lumpish. Monstrous, monstrous, and palpable, not to bee spoken of in a Christian Congregation: thou hast skumd ouer the Schoolemen, and of the froth of theyr folly, made a dish of diuinitie Brewesse, which the dogges will not eate. If the Printer haue any great dealings with thee, hee were best to get a priuiledge betimes, *Ad imprimendum solum*, forbidding all other to sell waste paper but himselfe, or else he will bee in a wofull taking. The Lambe of God make thee a wiser Bell-weather then thou art, for else I doubt thou wilt be driuen to leaue all and fall to thy fathers occupation, which is, to goe and make a rope to hang thy selfe. *Neque enim Lex æquior vlla est, quam necis artifices arte perire sua:* and so I leaue thee till a better opportunity, to bee tormented world without end, of our Poets and Writers about London, whome thou hast called piperlye Make-playes and Make-bates: not doubting but hee also whom thou tearmest the vaine *Paphatchet*, will haue a flurt at thee one day: all ioyntly driuing thee to this issue, that thou shalt bee constrained to go to the chiefe Beame of thy Benifice, and there beginning a lamentable speech with *cur scripsi, cur perii*, end with *parauum praua decent, iuuat inconcessa voluptas*, and so with a trice, trusse vp thy life in the string of thy Sancebell. So be it, pray Pen, Incke and paper on their knees, that they may not bee troubled with thee any more.

His owne words.

Redeo ad vos mei Auditores, haue I not a

indifferent prittye vayne in Spurgalling an Asse? if you knew how extemporall it were at this instant, and with what hast it is writ you would say so. But I would not haue you thinke that all this that is set downe heere, is in good earnest, for then you goe by S. *Gyles*, the wrong way to *Westminster:* but onely to shewe howe for a neede I could rayle, if I were throughly fyred. So ho, *Honiger / Ham-* [E1v] *mon*, where are you all this while, I cannot be acquainted with you? Tell me what doe you thinke of the case, am I subiect to the sinne of Wrath I write against or no, in whetting my penne on this blocke. I know you would faine haue it so, but it shall not choose but be otherwise for this once. Come on let vs turne ouer a new leafe, and heare what Gluttonie can say for her selfe, for Wrath hath spet his poyson, and full platters doe well after extreame purging.

THE Romaine Emperours that succeeded *Augustus*, were exceedingly giuen to this horrible vice, whereof some of them would feed on nothing but the tongues of Phesants and Nightingales: other, would spend as much at one banquet, as a kings reuenues came to in a yeare, whose excesse I would decypher at large, but that a new Laureat

The complaint of Gluttonie.

hath sau'd me the labor: who for a man that stands vpon paines and not wit, hath performd as much as any Storie dresser may doo, that sets a new English nap on an old Latine Apothegs. It is enough for me to licke dishes heere at home, though I feed not mine eyes at any of the *Romane* feasts. Much good doe it you Maister *Diues* heere in *London:* for you are he my pen meanes to dine withall. *Miserere mei*, what a fat churle it is? Why, he hath a belly as big as the round Church in *Cambridge*, a face as huge as the whole bodie of a base viall, and legs that if they were hollow, a man might keepe a mill in eyther of them. *Experto credo Roberto*, there is no mast like a Marchants table. *Bona fide*, it is a great misture, that we haue not men swine as well as beasts, for then we should haue porke that hath no more bones than a pudding, and a side of bacon that you might lay vnder your head in stead of a bolster.

Nature, in England is but plaine Dame, but in Spaine and Italy (because they haue more vse

It is not for nothing, that other Countries whom we vpbraide with Drunkennesse, call vs bursten-bellied Gluttons: for wee make our greedie paunches powdring tubs of beefe, and eat more meat at one meale, than the Spaniard or Italian in a moneth. Good thrifty mẽ, they draw out a dinner with sallets, like a *Swart-rutters* sute, and make *Madona* Nature their best Caterer. We must haue our Tables furnisht like Poulters stalls, or as though we were to victual *Noahs* Arke again (wherin there was al sorts of liuing creatures that euer were) or els the good-wife will not / open [E2 her mouth to bid one welcome. A stranger that should come to one of our *Magnificoes* houses, when dinner were set on the boord, and he not yet set, would thinke the goodman of the house were a Haberdasher of Wilde-fowle, or a Merchant venturer of daintie meate, that sels commodities of good cheere by the great, and hath Factors in *Arabia*, *Turkey*, *Egipt*, and *Barbarie*, to prouide him of straunge Birdes, *China* Mustard, and odde patterns to make Custards by.

of her than we) she is dubbed a Ladie.

Lord, what a coyle haue we with this Course and that course, remoouing this dish higher, setting another lower, and taking awaye the third. A Generall might in lesse space remooue his Campe, than they stand disposing of their gluttonie. And whereto tends all this gurmandise, but to giue sleepe grosse humors to feede on, to corrupt the braine, and make it vnapt and vnweldie for any thing.

The *Romane* Censors, if they lighted vpon a fat corpulent man, they straight tooke away his horsse, and constrained him to goe a foote:

positiuely concluding, his carkasse was so puft vp with gluttonie or idlenesse. If we had such horse-takers amongst vs, and that surfit-swolne Churles, who now ride on their foot-cloathes, might be constrained to carrie their flesh budgets from place to place on foote, the price of veluet and cloath would fall with their belies, and the gentle craft (*alias* the red herrings kinsmen) get more and drinke lesse. *Plenus venter nil agit libenter, & plures gula occidit quam gladius.* It is as desperate a peece of seruice, to sleepe vpon a full stomacke, as it is to serue in face of the bullet: a man is but his breath, and that may as well be stopt by putting too much in his mouth at once, as running on the mouth of the cannon. That is verefied of vs, which *Horace* writes of an outragious eater in his time, *Quicquid quæsierat ventri donabat auaro,* Whatsoeuer he could rap or rend, he confiscated to his couetous gut. Nay, we are such flesh-eating Saracens, that chast fish may not content vs, but we delight in the murder of innocent mutton, in the vnpluming of pullerie, and quartering of Calues and Oxen. It is horrible and detestable, no godly Fishmonger that can digest it. Report (which our moderners clippe flundring Fame) puts me in memorie of a notable iest I heard long a goe of Doctor

A rare wittie iest of Doctor Watson.

Watson, verye conducible to the reproofe of these / fleshly minded *Belials*. He beeing [E2v at supper on a fasting or fish night at least, with a great number of his friends and acquaintance, there chanced to be in the company an outlandish Doctor, who when all other fell to such victuals (agreeing to the time) as were before them, he out stript them, and there being one ioynt of flesh on the table for such as had weake stomackes, fell freshly to it. After that hunger (halfe conquered) had restored him to the vse of his speach, for his excuse he said to his friend that brought him thither, *Profecto Domine, ego sum malissimus piscator*, meaning by *piscator*, a Fishman: (which is a liberty, as also *malissimus*, that outlandish men in theyr familiar talke do challenge, at least vse aboue vs,) *At tu es bonissimus carnifex*, quoth Doctor *Watson*, retorting very merily his owne licentious figures vpon him. So of vs may it be said we are *Malissimi piscatores*, but *bonissimi carnifices*. I would English the iest for the edification of the temporalitie, but that it is not so good in English as in Latine: and though it were as good, it would not conuert clubs and clowted shoone from the flesh pots of *Egipt*, to the Prouant of the Lowe-countries, for they had rather (with the Seruingman) put vp a

Or rather Belly-als, because all their minde is on their belly.

Supplication to the Parliament house, that they might haue a yard of pudding for a penie, than desire (with the Baker) there might bee three ounces of bread sold for a halfe penie.

The moderation of Fryer Alphonso, K. Philips Confessor.

Alphonsus King *Phillips* Confessor, that came ouer with him to *England*, was such a moderate man in his dyet, that hee would feed but once a day, and at that time he would feed so slenderly and sparingly, as scarce serued to keepe life and soule together, one night importunately inuited to a solemne banquet, for fashion sake, he sate downe among the rest, but by no entreatie could be drawne to eate any thing: at length fruite beeing set on the boord, he reacht an apple out of the dish, and put it in his pocket, which one marking, that sat right ouer against him, askt him, *Domine cur es solicitus in crastinum? Sir, why are you carefull for the morrow?* Whereto he answered most soberly, *Imo hoc facio mi amice, vt ne sim solicitus in crastinum: No, I doo it my friend, that I may not be carefull for the morrow:* as though his appetite were a whole day contented with so little as an apple, and that it were enough to paye the morrowes tribute to Nature. / [E3

The strang alteration of the

Rare and worthy to be registred to all posterities, is the Countie *Molines* (sometime the Prince of *Parmaes* Companion) altred course of life, who being a man that liued in as great pompe and delicacie, as was possible for a man to doo, and one that wanted nothing but a kingdome that his heart could desire. Vpon a day entering into a deepe melancholy by himselfe, hee fell into a discoursiue consideration, what this world was, how vaine and transitory the pleasures thereof, and how manie times he had offended God by surfetting, gluttony, drunkennes, pride, whoredome and such like, and how hard it was for him that liu'd in that prosperitie that he did, not to bee entangled with those pleasures: whereupon he presently resolu'd twixt God and his owne conscience, to forsake it and al his allurements, and betake hime to the seuerest forme of life vsed in their state. And with that cald all his Souldiers and acquaintance together, and making knowen his intent vnto them, he distributed his liuing and possessions (which were infinite) amongst the poorest of them: and hauing not left himselfe the worth of one farthing vnder heauen, betooke him to the most beggerly new erected Order of the Fryer Capuchines. Their Institution is, that they shall possesse nothing whatsoeuer of their owne, more than the cloathes on their backes, continually go bare foote, weare haire shirts, and lie vpon the

Countie Molines, the Prince of Parmas Companion.

hard bords winter and summer time, they must haue no meate, nor aske any but what is giuen them voluntarily, nor must they lay vp from any meale to meale but giue it to the poore, or els it is a great penaltie. In this seuere humilitie liues this deuout Countie, and hath done this tweluemonth submitting himselfe to all the base drudgery of the house, as fetching water, making cleane the rest of their chambers, insomuch as he is the *Iunior* of the Order. O what a notable rebuke were his honourable Lowlines to succeeding pride, if this prostrate spirit of his were not the seruaunt of Superstition: or hee mispent not his good workes on a wrong Faith.

Let but our English belly-gods punish their pursie bodies with this strict penaunce, and professe Capuchinisme but one month, and Ile be their pledge they shall not grow so like dry-fats as they doo. O it will make them iolly long winded to trot vp and downe the Dorter staires, and the water-tankard wil / [E3v] keepe vnder the insurrection of their shoulders, the haire shirt will chase whordome out of their boanes, and the hard lodging on the boards take their flesh downe a button hole lower.

But if they might be induced to distribute all their goods amongst the poore, it were to be hoped Saint *Peter* would let them dwell in the suburbes of heauen, whereas other wise they must keepe aloofe at *Pancredge*, and not come neere the liberties by fiue leagues and aboue. It is your dooing (*Diotrephes* Diuell) that these stal-fed cormorants to damnation, must bung vp all the welth of the Land in their snaphaunce bags, and poore Scholers and Souldiers wander in backe lanes, and the out-shiftes of the Citie, with neuer a rag to their backes: but our trust is, that by some intemperance or other, you will turne vp their heeles one of these yeares together, and prouide them of such vnthrifts to their heires, as shall spend in one weeke amongst good fellowes, what they got by extortion and opression from Gentlemen all their life time.

The complaint of drunkennes.

FROM Gluttony in meates, let me discend to superfluitie in drinke: a sinne, that euer since we haue mixt our selues with the Low-countries, is counted honourable: but before we knew their lingring warres, was held in that highest degree of hatred that might be. Then if we had seene a man goe wallowing in the streetes, or line sleeping vnder the boord, we would haue spet at him as a toade, and cald him foule drunken swine, and warnd al our friends out of his company:

Drinking super nagulum, a deuise of drinking new come out of Fraunce; which is, after a man hath turnd vp the bottom of the cup, to drop it on his naile & make a pearle with that is left, which, if it shed & he cannot make stand on, by reason thers too much, he must drinke againe for his pennance.

now he is no body that cannot drinke *super nagulum*, carouse the Hunters hoop, quaffe *vpsey freze crosse*, with healthes, gloues, mumpes, frolickes, and a thousand such dominiering inuentions. He is reputed a pesaunt and a boore that wil not take his licour profoundly. And you shall heare a Caualier of the first feather, a princockes that was but a Page the other day in the Court, and now is all to be frenchified in his Souldiers sute, stand vppon termes with Gods wounds you dishonour me sir, you do me the disgrace if you do not pledge me as much as I drunke to you: and in the midst of his cups stand vaunting his manhood: beginning euerie sentence, with when I first bore Armes, when he neuer bare any thing but his Lords rapier after him in / his life. If he haue beene [E4 ouer and visited a towne of Garrison as a trauailer or passenger, he hath as great experience as the greatest Commander and chiefe Leader in *England*. A mightie deformer of mens manners and features, is this vnnecessary vice of all other. Let him bee indued with neuer so many vertues, and haue as much goodly proportion and fauour as nature can bestow vppon a man: yet if hee be thirstie after his owne destruction, and hath no ioy nor comfort, but when he is drowning his soule in a gallon pot, that one beastly imperfection, will vtterlie obscure all that is commendable in him: and all his good qualities sinke like lead down to the bottome of his carrowsing cups, where they will lie like lees and dregges, dead and vnregarded of any man.

Clim of the clough, thou that vsest to drinke nothing but scalding lead and sulpher in hell, thou art not so greedie of thy night gaere. O, but thou hast a foule swallow, if it come once to carousing of humane bloud, but thats but seldome once in seauen yeare, when theres a great execution, otherwise thou art tide at rack and manger, and drinkest nothing but the *Aqua vitæ* of vengeance all thy life time. The Prouerbe giues it forth, thou art a knaue, and therefore I haue more hope thou art some manner of good fellowe: let mee intreate thee (since thou hast other iniquities inough to circumuent vs withall) to wipe this sin out of the catologue of thy subtilties; helpe to blast the Vines that they may beare no more grapes, and sowre the wines in the cellers of Marchants storehouses, that our Countrey-men may not pisse out all their witte and thrift against the walles. King *Edgar*, because his subiects should not offend in swilling and bibbing, as they did, caused

King Edgars ordinance against drinking.

certaine yron-cups to be chained to euery fountaine and wells side, and at euery Vintners doore, with yron pinnes in them, to stinte euery man how much he should drinke: and he that went beyond one of those pinnes forfeited a penny for euery draught. And if Stories were well searcht, I beleeue hoopes in quart pots were inuented to that ende, that euery man should take his hoope, and no more. I haue heard it iustified for a trueth by great Personages, that the olde Marquesse of *Pisana* (who yet liues) drinkes not once in seauen yeare: and I haue read of one *Andron* of *Argos*, that / was so seldome thirstie, [E4v] that he trauailed ouer the hote burning sands of *Lybia*, and neuer dranke. Then why should our colde Clime bring foorth such fierie throates. Are we more thirstie than *Spaine* and *Italy* where the Sunnes force is doubled? The *Germaines* and lowe Dutch, me thinkes should bee continually keept moyst with the foggie aire and stinking mistes that arise out of their fennie soyle: but as their Countrey is ouer-flowen with water, so are their heads alwaies ouer-flowen with wine, and in their bellies they haue standing quag-mires and bogs of English beere.

The wonderful abstinence of the Marques of Pisana, yet liuing.

One of their breede it was that writ the Booke *De Arte bibendi:* a worshipfull treatise,

The priuat lawes amongst drunkards.

fitte for none but *Silenus* and his Asse to set forth: besides that volume, we haue generall rules and iniunctions, as good as printed precepts, or Statutes set downe by Acte of Parliament that goe from drunkard to drunkard; as still to keepe your first man, not to leaue any flockes in the bottome of the cup, to knock the glasse on your thumbe when you haue done, to haue some shooing horne to pul on your wine, as a rasher of the coles, or a redde herring, to stirre it about with a candles ende to make it taste better, and not to holde your peace whiles the pot is stirring.

Nor haue we one or two kinde of drunkards onely, but eight kindes. The first is Ape drunke, and he leapes, and sings, and hollowes, and daunceth for the heauens: the second is Lion drunke, and he flings the pots about the house, calls his Hostesse whore, breakes the glasse windowes with his dagger, and is apt to quarrell with any man that speaks to him: the third is Swine drunke, heauy, lumpish, and sleepie, and cries for a little more drinke, and a fewe more cloathes: the fourth is Sheepe drunke, wise in his owne conceipt, when he cannot bring foorth a right word, the fifth is Mawdlen drunke, when a fellowe will weepe for kindnes in the midst of his Ale, and kisse you, saying; By God

The eight kinds of drunkennesse.

Captaine I loue thee, goe thy waies thou dost not thinke so often of me as I do of thee, I would (if it pleased GOD) I could not loue thee so well as I doo, and then he puts his finger in his eie, and cries: the sixt is Martin drunke, when a man is drunke and drinkes himselfe sober ere he stirre: the seuenth is Goate drunke, when in his drunkennes he hath no minde / but on Lechery: the [F1 eighth is Foxe drunke, when he is craftie drunke, as many of the Dutch men bee, will neuer bargaine but when they are drunke. All these *species* and more I haue seene practised in one Company at one sitting, when I haue beene permitted to remaine sober amongst them, onely to note their seuerall humors. Hee that plies any one of them harde, it will make him to write admirable verses, to haue a deepe casting head, though hee were neuer so verie a Dunce before.

The discommodities of drunkennesse.

Gentlemen, all you that will not haue your braines twise sodden, your flesh rotten with the Dropsie, that loue not to goe in greasie dublets, stockings out at the heeles, and weare alehouse daggers at your backes, forsweare this slauering brauery, that will make you haue stinking breathes, and your bodies smell like Brewers aprons: rather keepe a snuffe in the bottome of the glasse to light you to bed withall, than leaue neuer an eye in your head to lead you ouer the threshould. It will bring you in your olde age to be companions with none but Porters and Car-men, to talke out of a Cage, railing as drunken men are wont, a hundred boies wondering about them; and to die sodainly as *Fol Long* the Fencer did, drinking *Aqua vitæ*. From which (as all the rest) good Lord deliuer *Pierce Penilesse*.

The complaint of Sloth.

THE nurse of this enormitie (as of all euills) is Idlenes or sloth, which hauing no painfull Prouince to set himselfe a worke, runnes headlong with the raines in his owne hand into all lasciuiousnesse and sensualitie that may be. Men when they are idle, and know not what to do, saith one let vs goe to the Stilliard and drinke Rhenish wine. Nay, if a man knew where a good whorhouse were saith another, it were somwhat like. Nay saith the third, let vs goe to a dicing-house or a bowling alley, and there we shall haue some sport for our money. To one of these three, (at hand quoth pick-purse) your euill Angelship maister mani-headed beast conducts them, *Vbi quid agitur* betwixt you and their soules be it, for I am no Drawer, Box-keeper, or Pander, to be priuie to their sports. If I were to paint Sloth, (as I am not seene in the sweetening) by Saint *Iohn* the / Euangelist [Fɪᵛ I sweare, I would draw it like a Stationer that I knowe, with his thumb vnder his girdle, who if a man come to his stall and aske him for a booke, neuer stirs his head, or looks vpon him, but stands stone still, and speakes not a word: onely with his little finger points backwards to his boy, who must be his interpreter, and so all the day gaping like a dumbe image he sits without motion, except at such times as he goes to dinner or supper: for then he is as quicke as other three, eating sixe times euery day. If I would raunge abroad, and looke in at sluggards key holes, I should finde a number lying a bed to saue charges of ordinaries, in winter when they want firing, losing halfe a weeks Commons together, to keepe them warme in the linnen. And hold you content, this Summer an vnder-meale of an afternoone long doth not amisse to exercise the eies withall. Fat men and Farmers sonnes that sweate much with eating harde cheese and drinking olde wine, must haue some more ease than yoong boyes that take their pleasure all day running vp and downe.

Videlicet, before he come out of his bed, then a set break-fast, then dinner, then after-noons nunch-ings, a supper and a rere-supper.

Setting iesting a side, I hold it a great disputable question which is a more euill man, of him that is an idle glutton at home, or a retchlesse vnthrift abroad? The glutton at home doth nothing but engender diseases, pamper his flesh vnto lust, and is good for none but his owne gut: the vnthrift abroad exerciseth his bodie at dauncing schoole, fence schoole, tennis, and all such recreations: the vintners, the victuallers, the dicing houses, and who not, get by him. Suppose he lose a little now and then at play, it teacheth him wit: and how should a man know to eschew vices, if his own experience did not acquaint him with their inconueniences? *Omne ignotum pro magnifico est:* that villany we haue made no assaies in, we admire. Besides, my vagrant Reueller haunts Plaies, & sharpens his wits with frequenting the company of Poets; he emboldens his blushing face by courting faire women on the sodaine, and looke into all Estates, by conuersing with them in publike places. Nowe tell me whether of these two, the heauie headed gluttonous house doue, or this liuelie wanton yoong Gallant, is like to prooue the wiser man, and better member in the Common-wealth. If my youth might not be thought partiall, the fine qualified Gentleman, although / [F2 vnstaide, should carrie it cleane away from the lazie clownish droane.

Which is better of the idle glutton, or vagrant vnthrift.

Sloath in Nobilitie, Courtiers, Schollers, or any men is the chiefest cause that brings them

The effects of sloth.

in contempt. For as industrie and vnfatigable toyle rayseth meane persons from obscure houses to high thrones of authoritie: so Sloath and sluggish securitye causeth proud Lords to tumble from the towers of their starrie discents, and be trod vnder foote of euery inferiour Besonian. Is it the loftie treading of a Galliard, or fine grace in telling of a loue tale amongst Ladies, can make a man reuerenst of the multitude? no, they care not for the false glistering of gay garments, or insinuating curtesie of a carpet Peere: but they delight to see him shine in armour, and oppose himselfe to honourable daunger,. to participate a voluntarie penurie with his Souldiers, and relieue part of their wants out of his owne purse. That is the course he that will be popular must take, which if he neglect, and sit dallying at home, nor will be awakt by any indignities out of his loue-dreame, but suffer euery vpstart groome to defie him, set him at naught, and shake him by the beard vnreuengde, let him straight take orders, and be a Church-man, and then his patience may passe for a vertue: but otherwise, he shall be suspected of cowardise, and not car'd for of any. The onely enemie to Sloth is contention and emulation; as to propose one man to my selfe, that is the onely myrrour of our Age,

The means to auoyde Sloth.

and striue to out-go him in vertue. But this strife must be so tempered, that we fall not from the eagernesse of praise, to the enuying of their persons: for then wee leaue running to the goale of glorie, to spurne at a stone that lyes in our waye; and so did *Atlanto* in the middest of her course, stoope to take vp the golden Apple that her enemie scattered in her way, and was out-runne by *Hippomenes*. The contrarie to this contention and emulation, is securitie, peace, quiet, tranquillitie, when we haue no aduersarie to prie into our actions, no malicious eye, whose pursuing our priuate behauiour, might make vs more vigilant ouer our imperfections, than otherwise we would be.

That State or Kingdome that is in league with all the world, and hath no forraine sword to vexe it, is not halfe so strong or confirmed to endure, as that which liues euery houre in feare of in- / uasion. There is a certaine [F2v waste of the people for whome there is no vse, but warre: and these men must haue some employment still to cut them off: *Nam si foras hostem non habent, domi inuenient.* If they haue no seruice abroad, they will make mutinies at home. Or if the affayres of the State be such, as cannot exhale all these corrupt excrements, it is very expedient they haue some light toyes to busie their heads withall, cast before them as bones to gnaw vpon, which may keepe them from hauing leisure to intermeddle with higher matters.

The defence of Playes.

To this effect, the pollicie of Playes is very necessary, howsoeuer some shallow-braind censures (not the deepest serchers into the secrets of gouernment) mightily oppugne them. For whereas the after-noone beeing idlest time of the day; wherein men that are their owne masters, (as Gentlemen of the Court, the Innes of the Courte, and the number of Captaines and Souldiers about *London*) do wholy bestow themselues vpon pleasure, and that pleasure they deuide (howe vertuously it skils not) either into gameing, following of harlots, drinking, or seeing a Playe: is it not then better (since of foure extreames all the world cannot keepe them but they will choose one) that they should betake them to the least, which is Playes? Nay, what if I prooue Playes to be no extreame: but a rare exercise of vertue? First, for the subiect of them (for the most part) it is borrowed out of our English Chronicles, wherein our forefathers valiant acts (that haue line long buried in rustie brasse, and worme-eaten bookes) are reuiued, and they themselues raised from the Graue of Obliuion, and brought to pleade their aged Honours in open presence: than which, what can be a sharper reproofe to these degenerate effeminate dayes of ours.

How would it haue ioyed braue *Talbot* (the terror of the French) to thinke that after he had lyne two hundred yeares in his Tombe, hee should triumphe againe on the Stage, and haue his bones newe embalmed with the teares of ten thousand spectators at least, (at seuerall times) who in the Tragedian that represents his person, imagine they behold him fresh bleeding.

I will defend it against any Collian, or clubfisted Vsurer of them all, there is no immortalitie, can be giuen a man on earth / [F3 like vnto Playes. What talke I to them of immortalitie, that are the onely vnderminers of Honour, and doe enuie any man that is not sprung vp by base Brokerie like themselues. They care not if all the auncient houses were rooted out, so that like the Burgomasters of the Low-countries they might share the gouernment amongst them as States, and be quarter-maisters of our Monarchie. All Artes to them are vanitie: and if you tell them what a glorious thing it is to haue *Henrie* the fifth represented on the Stage leading the French King prisoner, and forcing both him and the

Dolphin to sweare fealty. I, but (will they say) what do we get by it? Respecting neither the right of Fame that is due to true Nobilitie deceased, nor what hopes of eternitie are to be proposed to aduentrous mindes, to encourage them forward, but onely their execrable luker, and filthie vnquenchable auarice.

They know when they are dead they shall not be brought vpon the Stage for any goodnes, but in a merriment of the Vsurer and the Diuel, or buying Armes of the Herald, who giues them the Lyon without tongue, tayle, or tallents, because his maister whome hee must serue is a Townesman, and a man of peace, and must not keepe any quarrelling beasts to annoy his honest neighbours.

The vse of Playes.

In Playes, all coosonages, all cunning drifts ouer-guylded with outward holinesse, all stratagems of warre, all the cankerwormes that breede on the rust of peace, are most liuely anatomiz'd: they shew the ill successe of treason, the fall of hastie climbers, the wretched end of vsurpers, the miserie of ciuill dissention, and how iust God is euermore in punishing of murther. And to proue euery one of these allegations, could I propound the circumstances of this play and that play, if I meant to handle this Theame otherwise than *obiter*. What should I say more? they are sower pils of reprehension wrapt vp in sweete words. Whereas some Petitioners of the Counsaile against them obiect, they corrupt the youth of the Cittie, and withdrawe Prentises from theyr worke; they heartily wishe they might bee troubled with none of their youth nor their prentises; for some of them (I meane the ruder handicrafts seruants) neuer come abroade, but they are in danger of vndoing: and as for corrupting them when / they come, thats false; for no Play they [F3v haue, encourageth any man to tumults or rebellion, but layes before such the halter and the gallowes; or praiseth or approoueth pride, lust, whoredome, prodigalitie, or drunkennes, but beates them downe vtterly. As for the hindrance of Trades and Traders of the Citie by them, that is an Article foysted in by the Vintners, Alewiues, and Victuallers, who surmise if there were no Playes, they should haue all the companie that resort to them, lye bowzing and beere-bathing in their houses euery after-noone. Nor so, nor so, good brother bottle-ale, for there are other places besides where money can bestow it selfe: the signe of the smock will wipe your mouth cleane; and yet I haue heard yee haue made her a tenant to your tap-houses. But what shall hee doo that hath spent himselfe? where

The confutation of Citizens obiections against Players.

shall hee haunt? Faith, when Dice, Lust, and Drunkennesse, and all haue dealt vpon him, if there be neuer a Playe for him to goe too for his pennie, he sits melancholie in his Chamber, deuising vpon felonie or treason, and howe he may best exalt himselfe by mischiefe.

In *Augustus* time (who was the Patron of all wittie sports) there happened a great Fraie in *Rome* about a Player, insomuch as all the Cittie was in an vprore: wherevpon, the Emperour (after the broyle was somewhat ouer-blowne) calde the Player before him, and askt what was the reason that a man of his qualitie, durst presume to make such a brawle about nothing. Hee smilinglye replyde, *It is good for thee O Cæsar, that the peoples heads are troubled with brawles and quarrels about vs and our light matters: for otherwise they would looke into thee and thy matters.* Read *Lipsius* or any prophane or Christian Polititian, and you shall finde him of this opinion.

A Players wittie answere to Augustus.

Our Players are not as the players beyond sea, a sort of squirting baudie Comedians, that haue whores and common Curtizens to playe womens partes, and forbeare no immodest speech, or vnchast action that may procure laughter, but our Sceane is more statelye furnisht than euer it was in the time of *Roscius*, our representations

A comparison twixt our Plaiers and the Players beyond the Sea.

honourable, and full of gallant resolution, not consisting like theirs of Pantaloun, a Whore, and a Zanie, but of Emperours, Kings and Princes: whose true Tragedies (*Sophocleo cothurno*) they do vaunt. / [F4

Not *Roscius* nor *Æsope* those admyred tragedians that haue liued euer since before Christ was borne, could euer performe more in action, than famous *Ned Allen*. I must accuse our Poets of sloth and partialitie that they will not boast in large impressions what worthy men (aboue all Nations) *England* affoords. Other Countries cannot haue a Fidler breake a string, but they will put it in print, and the old *Romanes* in the writings they published, thought scorne to vse any but domestical examples of their owne hom-bred Actors, Schollers and Champions, and them they would extoll to the third and fourth Generation: Coblers ,Tinkers, Fencers, none escapt them, but they mingled them all in one Gallimafrey of glory.

The due commendation of Ned Allen.

Heere I haue vsed a like Method, not of tying my selfe to mine owne Countrie, but by insisting in the experience of our time: and if I euer write any thing in Latine, (as I hope one day I shall) not a man of any desert here amongst vs, but I will haue vp. *Tarlton*, *Ned Allen*, *Knell*, *Bentlie*, shall be made knowne to

France, *Spaine*, and *Italie*: and not a part that they surmounted in, more than other, but I will there note and set downe, with the manner of theyr habites and attyre.

The seuenth and last complaint of Lecherie.

THE childe of Sloath is Lecherie, which I haue plac't last in my order of handling: a sinne that is able to make a man wicked that should describe it; for it hath more starting holes, than a siue hath holes, more Clyents than *Westminster-hall*, more diseases than *Newgate*. Call a Leete at *Byshopsgate*, and examine how euery second house in *Shorditch* is maintayned: make a priuie search in *Southwarke*, and tell me how many Shee-Inmates you finde: naye, goe where you will in the Suburbes, and bring me two Virgins that haue vowd Chastitie, and Ile builde a Nunnerie.

Westminster, *Westminster*, much maydenhead hast thou to answere for at the day of Iudgement, thou hadst a Sanctuarie in thee once, but hast few Saints left in thee now. Surgeons and Apothecaries, you know what I speake is true: for you liue (like Sumners) vpon the sinnes of the people; tell me, is there anye place so lewde as this Ladie *London?* not a Wench sooner creepes out of the shell, but she is of the Religion. Some wiues / will [F4v sowe Mandrake in their gardens, and crosse-neighborhood with them is counted good-fellowship.

The Court I dare not touch, but surely there (as in the Heauens) be many falling starres, and but one true *Diana*. *Consuetudo peccandi, tollit sensum peccati*, Custome is a Lawe, and Luste holdes it for a Lawe, to liue without Lawe. *Lais* that had so manie Poets to her Louers, could not alwayes preserue her beauty with their praises. Marble will weare away with much raine: Gold will rust with moyst keeping; and the richest garments are subiect to Times Moath-frets, *Clitemnestra*, that slew her husband to enioye the Adulterer *Ægistus*, and bathde her selfe in Milke euery day to make her yoong againe, had a time when shee was ashamed to viewe her selfe in a looking Glasse, and her body withered, her minde being greene. The people pointed at her for a murtherer, yoong children howted at her as a strumpet: shame, misery, sicknesse, beggery, is the best end of vncleannesse.

Lais, *Cleopatra*, *Helen*, if our Clyme hath any such, noble Lord warden of the witches and iuglers, I commend them with the rest of our vncleane sisters in *Shorditch*, the *Spittle*, *Southwarke*, *Westminster*, *&* *Turnbull streete*, to the protection of your Portership: hoping you will speedily carrie them to hell, there to keepe open house for all young Diuels that come, and not let our ayre bee contaminated with theyr six-pennie damnation any longer.

Your Diuelships
bounden execrator,

Pierce Penilesse. /

[G1

A Supplication calst thou this, (quoth the Knight of the post) it is the maddest Supplication that euer I sawe; me thinks thou hast handled all the seuen deadly sinnes in it, and spared none that exceedes his limits in any of them. It is well done to practise thy witte, but (I beleeue) our Lord will cun thee little thanks for it.

The worse for me (quoth I) if my destinie be such, to lose my labour euery where, but I meane to take my chance be it good or bad. Well, hast thou any more that thou wouldest haue mee to doo (quoth he?) Onely one sute (quoth I) which is this, that sith opportunitie so conuenientlie serues, you would acquaint mee with the state of your infernall regiment: and what that hel is, where your Lord holdes his throne; whether a world like this, which spirites like outlawes doo inhabit, who being banisht from heauen, as they are from their Country, enuy that any shall bee more happy than they: and therefore seeke all meanes possible that Wit or Arte may inuent, to make other men as wretched as themselues: or, whether it be place of horror, stench, and darknesse, where men see meat, but can get none, or are euer thirstie and readie to swelt for drinke, yet haue not the power to taste the coole streames that runne hard at their feet:

where (*permutata vicissitudine*) one ghost torments another by turnes, and he that all his life time was a great fornicator, hath all the diseases of lust continually hanging vppon him, and is constrained (the more to augment his misery) to haue congresse euery houre with hagges and olde witches: and he that was a great drunkard here on earth, hath his penance assigned him, to carouse himselfe drunke with dishwash and Vineger, and surfet foure times a day, with sower Ale and small Beere: as so of the rest, as the vsurer to swallow moulten gold, the glutton to eate nothing but toades, and the Murtherer to bee still stabd with daggers, but neuer die: or whether (as some phantasticall refyners of philosophie will needes perswade vs) hell is nothing but error, and that none but fooles and Idiotes and Machanicall men that haue no learning shall be damned: of these doubts if you will resolue me, I shall thinke my selfe to haue profited greatly by your company.

He hearing me so inquisitiue in matters aboue humane / capacity, entertained my [G1v greedie humour with this answere. Poets and Philosophers that take a pride in inuenting newe opinions, haue sought to renoume their wittes, by hunting after strange conceits of heauen and hell; all generally agreeing, that such places there are, but how inhabited, by whom gouerned, or what betides them that are transported to the one or other, not two of them iumpe in one tale. We that to our terror and griefe do know their dotage by our sufferings, reioyce to thinke how these sillie flyes plaie with the fire that must burne them.

But leauing them to the Laborynth of their fond curiositie, shall I tell thee in a word what Hell is? It is a place where the soules of vntemperate men and ill liuers of all sorts, are detayned and imprisoned till the generall Resurrection, kept and possessed chiefly by spirites, who lye like Souldiours in Garison, ready to be sent about any seruice into the world, whensoeuer *Lucifer* their Lieftenaunt Generall pleaseth. For the scituation of it in respect of heauen, I can no better compare it than to *Callis* and *Douer*: for as a man standing vpon *Callis* Sands may see men walking on *Douer* Clyffes, so easily may you discerne Heauen from the farthest part of hell, and behold the melodie and motions of the Angels and Spirits there resident, in such perfect manner, as if you were amongst them; which how it worketh in the mindes and soules of them that haue no power to apprehend such felicity, it is not for me to intimate, because it is preiudiciall to our Monarchie.

I would bee sorrie (quoth I) to importune you in anie matter of secrecie: yet this I desire, if it might bee done without offence, that you would satisfie me in full sort and according to truth, what the Diuell is whome you serue? as also howe he began, and howe farre his power and authoritie extends?

Persie, beleeue me thou shriuest me very neere in this latter demaund, which concerneth vs more deeply than the former, and may worke vs more damage than thou art aware of: yet in hope thou wylt conceale what I tell thee, I will laye open our whole estate plainly and simply vnto thee as it is: but first I wil begin with the opinions of former times, and so hasten forwarde / to that *manifeste* [G2 *verum* that thou seekest. Some men there be that building too much vpon reason, perswade themselues, that there are no Diuels at all; but that this word *Dæmon*, is such another morall of mischiefe, as the Poets Dame Fortune is of mishap: for as vnder the fiction of this blinde Goddesse we ayme at the folly of Princes and great men in disposing of honours, that oftentimes preferre fooles and disgrace wise men, and alter their fauours in turning of an eye, as Fortune turnes her wheele: so vnder the person of this olde *Gnathonicall* companion called the Diuell, we shrowd all subtilitie masking vnder the name of simplicitie, all painted holines deuouring widowes houses, all gray headed Foxes clad in sheepes garments; so that the Diuell (as they make it) is onely a pestilent humour in a man, of pleasure, profit, or policie, that violently carries him away to vanitie, villanie, or monstrous hypocrisie: vnder vanitie I comprehend not onely all vaine Arts and studies whatsoeuer, but also dishonourable prodigalitie, vntemperate venery, and that hatefull sinne of selfe-loue, which is so common amongst vs: vnder villanie I comprehend murder, treason, theft, cousnage, cut-throat couetise, and such like: lastly, vnder hypocrisie, all Machiauilisme, puritanisme, and outward gloasing with a mans enemie, and protesting friendship to him that I hate, and meane to harme: all vnder-hand cloaking of bad actions with Common-wealth pretences: and finally all Italionate conueyances, as to kill a man, and then mourne for him, *quasi vero* it was not by my consent, to be a slaue to him that hath iniur'd me, and kisse his feete for opportunitie of reuenge, to be seuere in punishing offenders, that none might haue the benefite of such meanes but my selfe, to vse men for my purpose and then cast them off, to seeke his destruction that knowes my secrets: and such as I haue imployed in any murther or stratagem, to set them priuilie together by the eares, to stab each other mutually, for feare of bewraying me: or if that faile, to hire them to humor one another in such courses, as may bring them both to the gallowes. These and a thousand more such sleights hath hypocrisie learned by trauailing strange Countries. I will not say she puts them in practise here in *England*, although there be as many false brethren and crafty knaues here / amongst vs, as in any [G2*v* place: witnes the poore Miller of *Cambridge*, that hauing no roome for his hen-loft, but the Testor of his bed, and it was not possible for any hungry Poultrers to come there, but they must stande vppon the one side of it, and so not steale them but with great hazard; had in one night notwithstanding (when hee and his wife were a snorting) all the whole progenie of their Pullery taken away, and neither of them heard any sturring: it is an odde tricke, but what of that, we must not stand vpon it, for wee haue grauer matters in hand, then the stealing of Hennes. Hypocrisie I remember was our Text, which was one of the chiefe morall Diuels our late Doctors affirme to bee most busie in these daies, and busie it is in trueth more than any Bee that I know: nowe you talke of a Bee, Ile tell you a tale of a Battle-dore.

The Beare on a time beeing chiefe Burgo-master of all the Beasts vnder the Lyon, gan thinke with himselfe how hee might surfet in pleasure, or best husband his Authoritie to enlarge his delight and contentment. Wyth that hee beganne to prye and to smell through euery corner of the Forrest for praye, to haue a thousande imagynations with him-selfe what daintie morsell he was master of, and yet had not tasted: whole Heards of sheepe had hee deuoured, and was not satisfied; fat Oxen, Hayfers, Swine, Calues, and yoong Kiddes, were his ordinary vyands: he longed for Horse-flesh, and went presently to a medowe, where a fat Cammell was grazing, whom fearing to encounter with force because he was a huge beast and well shod, he thought to betray vnder the colour of demaunding homage, hoping that as he should stoope to doo him truage, he might seaze vpon his throat and stifle him before he should be able to recouer himselfe from his false embrace; but therein he was deceiued: for comming vnto this stately Beast with this imperious message, in stead of doing homage vnto him, he lifted vp one of his hindmost heeles, and stroake him such a blowe on the forehead that hee ouerthrew him. Thereat not a little mou'd and enrag'd, that he should be so dishonored by his inferiour as he thought, he consulted with the Ape how he might be reuenged.

The Ape abhorring him by nature, because he ouerlookt / him so Lordly, and was by [G3 so many degrees greater than he was, aduised him to digge a pit with his pawes right in the way where this big boand Gentleman should passe, that so stumbling and falling in, he might lightly skip on his back, and bridle him, and then he come and seaze on him at his pleasure. No sooner was this perswaded, than performed: for enuie that is neuer idle, could not sleepe in his wrath, or ouer-slip the least opportunitie, till hee had seene the confusion of his enemie. Alas goodly Creature, that thou mightest no longer liue. What auaileth thy gentlenes, thy prowesse, or the plentifull pasture, wherein thou wert fed: since malice triumphs ouer all thou commaundest? Well may the Mule rise vp in armes, and the Asse bray at the Authors of thy death: yet shall their furie be fatall to themselues, before it take hold on these Traitours. What needeth more words? the deuourer feedes on his captiue, and is gorged with bloud. But as auarice and crueltie are euermore thirstie, so far'd it with this hungrie Vsurper: for hauing flesht his ambition with this treacherous conquest, he past a long through a groue, where a Heard of Deare weare a ranging: whom when he had stedfastly surueyed from the fattest to the leanest, he singled out one of the fairest of the company, with whom he meant to close vp his stomack in stead of cheese: but because the Wood-men were euer stirring thereabout, and it was not possible for one of his coate, to commit such outrage vndescried, and that if he were espyed, his life were in perill: though not with the Lyon, whose eyes he could blinde as hee list, yet with the lesser sort of the brutish Comminaltie, whome no flatterie might pacifie. Therefore he determined slylie and priuilie to poyson the streame, where this iolly Forrester wonted to drinke; and as he determined, so he did: whereby it fell out, that when the Sunne was ascended to his height, and all the nimble Cittizens of the Wood betooke them to their Laire, this youthfull Lorde of the Lawnds, all fainte and malecontent (as prophecying his neere approching mishap by his languishing) with a lazie wallowing pace, strayed aside from the rest of his fellowship, and betooke him all carelesly to the corrupted fountaine that was prepared for his Funerall.

Ah, woe is me, this poyson is pittilesse. What neede I saye more, since you know it is death with whome it encounters. And / [G3v yet cannot all this expence of life, set a period to insatiable Murther: but still it hath some Anuile to worke vppon, and ouer-casts all opposite prosperitie, that may any waye shadow his glorie.

Too long it were to rehearse all the practises of this sauadge blood-hunter, how he assailed the Vnicorne as he slept in his den, and tore the heart out of his breast ere he could awake: how hee made the lesser beasts lye in wayte one for the other, and the Crocodyle to coape with the Basiliske, that when they had enterchangeably weakened each other, he might come and insult ouer them both as hee list. But these were lesser matters, which daily vse had worne out of mens mouthes, and he himselfe had so customablie practised, that often exercise had quite abrogated the opinion of sinne, and impudencie throughlie confirmed an vndaunted defiance of vertue in his face. Yet newfangled lust, that in time is wearie of welfare, and will bee as soone cloyed with too much ease and delicacie, as Pouertie with labour and scarcitie, at length brought him out of loue with this greedy bestiall humour:

and nowe hee affected a milder varietie in his dyet: hee had bethought him what a pleasant thing it was to eate nothing but honie another while, and what great store of it there was in that Countrey.

Nowe did hee cast in his head, that if hee might bring the Husbandmen of the soyle in opinion, that they might buie honey cheaper, than beeing at such charges in keeping of Bees, or that those Bees which they kept, were most of them Drones, and what should such idle Drones doe with such stately Hyues, or lye sucking at such pretious Honny-combes; that if they were tooke awaye from them, and distributed equally abroade, they would releeue a great many of painfull labourers that had neede of them, and would continually liue seruiceable at theyr commaund, if they might enioy such a benefite. Naye more, let them giue Waspes but onely the waxe, and dispose of the honie as they thinke good, and they shall humme and buzze a thousand times lowder than they, and haue the hiue fuller at the yeares ende (with young ones I meane) than the Bees are woont in ten yeere.

To broach this deuice, the Foxe was addrest like a shepheards / dogge, and [G4 promist to haue his Pattent seald, to be the

Kings Poulterer for euer, if he could bring it to passe. Faith, quoth he, and Ile put it in a venter, let it hap how it wil. With that he grew in league with an old Camelion, that could put on all shapes, and imitate any colour, as occasion serued, and him he addrest sometime like an Ape to make sport, and then like a Crocodile to weep, sometime like a Serpent to sting, and by and by like a Spaniell to fawne, that with these sundrie formes, (applyde to mens variable humors) he might perswade the world he ment as he spake, and onely intended their good, when he thought nothing lesse. In this disguise, these two deceiuers went vp and downe, and did much harme vnder the habite of Simplicity, making the poore silly Swaines beleeue they were cunning Phisitions, and well seene in all Cures, that they could heale any maladie, though neuer so daungerous, and restore a man to life that had beene dead two daies, onely by breathing vpon him: aboue all things they perswaded them, that the honny that their Bees brought foorth, was poysonous and corrupt, by reason that those floures and hearbs, out of which it was gathered and exhaled, were subiect to the infection of euery Spider and venimous Canker, and not a loathsome Toade (how detestable soeuer) but reposde himselfe vnder theyr shadow, and lay sucking at their rootes continually: wheras in other Countries, no noisome or poisnous creature might liue, by reason of the imputed goodnes of the Soyle, or carefull diligence of the Gardners aboue ours, as for example, *Scotland*, *Denmarke*, and some more pure partes of the seauenteene Prouinces.

These perswasions made the good honest Husbandmen to pause, and mistrust their owne wits very much, in nourishing such dangerous Animals, but yet I know not how antiquitie and custome so ouer-rulde their feare, that none would resolue to abandon them on the sodaine, till they sawe a further inconuenience: whereby my two cunning Philosophers were driuen to studie *Galen* a new, and seeke out splenatiue simples, to purge their popular Patients of the opinion of their olde Traditions and Customes: which howe they wrought with the most parte that had least wit, it were a world to tell. For now nothing was Canonical but what they speake, no man would conuerse with his wife, but / first askt their aduise, nor pare his nailes, [G4v nor cut his beard, without their prescription: so senceles, so wauering is the light vnconstant multitude, that will daunce after euerie mans pipe; and sooner prefer a blind harper that can squeake out a new horne-pipe, than *Alcinous* or *Apolloes* varietie, that imitates the right straines of the *Doryan* melodie. I speake this to amplifie the nouell folly of the hedlong vulgar, that making their eyes and eares vassailes to the legerdemaine of these iugling Mountbanks, are presentlie drawne to contemne Art and experience in comparison of the ignorance of a number of audatious idiots. The Fox can tell a faire tale, and couers all his knauerie vnder conscience, and the Camelion can addresse himself like an Angell whensoeuer he is disposed to worke mischefe by myracles: but yet in the end their secret drifts are laide open, and *Linceus* eyes that see through stone walles, haue made a passage into the close couerture of their hypocrisie.

For one daie, as these two Deuisers were plotting by themselues how to driue all the Bees from their Honny combs, by putting wormwood in their Hyues, and strewing Henbane and Rue in euerie place where they resort: a Flye that past by, and heard all their talke, stomaking the Foxe of olde, for that he had murdred so many of his kindred with his flail-driuing tail, went presentlie and buzd in *Linceus* eares the whole purport of their malice, who awaking his hundred eies at these vnexpected tidings, gan persue them wheresoeuer they went, and trace their intents as they proceeded into action, so that ere half their baits were cast forth, they were apprehended and imprisoned, and all their whole counsaile detected. But long ere this, the Beare impatient of delaies and consumed with an inward greife in himselfe, that hee might not haue his will of a fat Hind that outran him, he went into the woods all melancholie, and there died for pure anger: leauing the Foxe and the Camelion to the destinie of their desert, and mercie of their Iudges. How they scape I know not, but some saie they were hanged, and so weele leaue them.

How likest thou of my tale friend *Persie*? Haue I not described a right earthly Diuell vnto thee, in the discourse of this bloodie minded Beare? Or canst thou not attract the true image of / hypocrisie, vnder the [H1 description of the Fox and the Camelion?

Yes very well (quoth I) but I would gladly haue you returne to your first subiect, since you haue mooued doubts in my mind, which you haue not yet discust.

Of the sundrie opinions of the Diuill thou meanest, and them that imagin him to haue no existence, of which sort are they that first inuented the prouerbe, *Homo homini Dæmon:*

meaning thereby, that that power which we call the Diuill, and the ministring Spirits belonging to him and to his kingdom, are tales and fables, and meere bugge-bearers to scarre boies: and that there is no such essence at all, but only it is a terme of large content, describing the rancor, grudg, and bad dealing of one man toward another: as namely, when one friend talkes with another subtilly, and seeks to diue into his commoditie, that he may depriue him of it craftelie: when the sonne seeks the death of the father, that he maie be infeoffed in his welth: and the stepdame goes about to make awaie her sonne in-law, that her children may inherit: when brothers fall at iarres for portions, and shall by open murther or priuie conspiracie, attempt the confusion of each other, only to ioine house to house, and vnite two Liuelihoods in one: when the seruant shall rob his master, and Men put in trust start away from their oathes and vowes they care not how.

In such cases and manie more, may one man be said to be a diuell to another, and this is the second opinion. The third is that of *Plato*, who not onely affirmeth that there are diuels, but deuided them into three sorts, euerie one a degree of dignitie aboue the other; the first are those, whose bodies are compact of the purest airie Element, combined with such transparant threeds; that neither they doo partake so much fire as should make them visible to sight, or haue anie such affinitie with the earth, as they are able to be prest or toucht: and these he setteth in the hiest incomprehensible degree of heauen. The second, he maketh these whom *Apuleius* doth call reasonable creatures, passiue in mind and eternall in time, being those *Apostata* spirits that rebelled with *Belzebub*: whose bodies, before their fall, were bright and pure all like to the former: but after their transgression, they were obscured with a thick ayrie matter & euer after assigned to darknes. The third, he attributes to those men, that by some / [H1v] diuine knowledgc or vnderstanding, seeming to aspire aboue mortalitie, are called *Dæmona*, (that is) *Gods*: for this word *Dæmon* contayneth either, and *Homer* in euery place doth vse it, both for that omnipotent power that was before al things, and the euill spirit that leadeth men to error: so doth *Syrianus* testifie, that *Plato* was called *Dæmon*, because he disputed of deepe Common-welth matters, greatly auailable to the benefite of his Countrye: and also *Aristotle* because he wrote at large of all things subiect to moouing and sence. Then belike (quoth I) you make this word *Dæmon*, a capeable name of Gods, of men and of diuels, which is farre distant from the scope of my demand: for I doo onlie inquire of the diuel, as this common appellation of the Diuel, signifieth a malignant spirit, enimie to mankind, and a hater of God and all goodnes. Those are the second kinde said he, vsuallie termed detractors or accusers that are in knowledge infinit, insomuch as by the quicknes of their wits, and agreeable mixtures of the Elements, they so comprehend those seminarie vertues to men vnknown, that those thinges which in course of time, or by growing degrees Nature of it selfe can effect. They by their Art and skill in hastening the works of nature, can contriue and compas in a moment, as the Magitians of *Pharao*, who wheras nature not without some interposition of time, and ordinarie causes of conception brings forth frogs, serpents, or any liuing thing else, they without all such distance of space, or circumscription of season euen in a thought assoon as their K. commanded, couered the land of *Aegypt* with this monstrous increase. Of the originall of vs spirits, the scripture most amplie maketh mention, namelie that *Lucifer* (before his fall) an Archangel, was a cleer bodie compact of the purest, and brightest of the aire; but after his fall, he was vailed with a grosser substance, and tooke a new forme of darke and thick ayre, which he still reteineth. Neither did he onlie fall, when he stroue with *Michael*, but drew a number of Aungels to his faction; who ioint partakers of his proud reuolt, were likewise partakers of his punishmente, and all thrust out of heauen togither by one iudgement: who euer since do nothing but wander about the Earth, and tempt and inforce fraile men to enterprise all wickednesse that maie be, and commit / most horrible and ab- [H2 hominable things against God. Maruell not that I discouer so much of our estate vnto thee: for the scripture hath more than I mention, as S. *Peter* where he saith that *God spared not his Angels that sinned.* And in another place where he saith, that *they are bound with the chaines of darknes, and throwne headlong into hell:* which is not meant of anie locall place in the earth, or vnder the waters: for as *Austin* affirmeth, we doo inhabite the Region vnder the moone, and haue the thick aire assigned vs as a prison, from whence we maie with small labour cast our nets where we list: yet are we not so at our disposition but that we are still commanded by *Lucifer* (although we are in number infinite) who retaining that pride wherewith he arrogantlie affected the maiestie of God, hath still his ministring Angels about him, whome he emploies in seuerall charges, to seduce and deceiue as him seemeth best: as those spirites which the Latines call *Iouios* and *Antemeridianos*, to speake out of Oracles, and make the people worship them as gods, when they are nothing but deluding Diuels that couet to haue a false Deitie ascribed vnto them, and drawe men vnto their loue by wonders & prodigies, that else would hate them deadlie, if they knew their maleuolence and enuie. Such a monarchizing spirit it was, that said to Christ, *If thou wilt fall downe and worship me, I wil giue thee al the kingdoms of the earth:* and such a spirit it was that possest the *Libian Sapho*, and the Emperor *Dioclesian*, who thought it the blessedest thing that might be, to be called God. For the one being wearie of humane honour, and inspired with a supernaturall follie, taught little birds that were capable of speech, to pronounce distinctlie *Magnus Deus Sapho*, that is to saie *A great God is Sapho:* Which words when they had learned readilie to caroll, & were perfect in their note, he let them flie at randon, that so dispersing themselues euerie where, they might induce the people to account of him as a God. The other was so arrogant, that he made his subiectes fall prostrate on their faces, and lifting vp their handes to him as to heauen, adore him as omnipotent.

The second kind of Deuils which he most imploieth, are those Northerne *Marcij*, called the spirits of reuenge, & the authors of massacres, and seedesmen of mischiefe, for they haue com- / mission to incense men [H2v to rapines, sacriledge, theft, murther, wrath, furie, and all manner of cruelties, and they commande certein of the Southern spirits (as slaues) to waite vpon them, as also great *Arioch*, that is tearmed the spirit of reuenge.

These know how to dissociate the loue of brethren, and to break wedlock bands with such violence, that they may not be vnited, and are prodominant in manie other domisticall mutinies: of whom if thou list to heare more, read the 39. of *Ecclesiasticus*. The Prophet *Esay* maketh menteon of another Spirit sent by God to the *Egyptians*, to make them straie and wander out of the way, that is to say, the Spirit of liing, which they call *Bolychym*. The Spirits that entice men to gluttonie and lust, are certaine watry spirits of the West, and certaine Southerne spirits as *Nefrach* & *Kelen*, which for the most part prosecute vnlawfull loues, and cherish all vnnaturall desires: they wander through lakes, fish ponds and fennes, and ouerwhelme ships, cast boates vpon ankers, and drowne men that are swimming: therefore are they counted the most pestilent, troublesome, and guilefull spirits that are: for by the helpe of *Alrynach* a Spirite of the West, they will raise stormes, cause earthquaks, whirlwinds, raine, haile or snow in the clerest daie that is: and if euer they appeare to anie man, they come in womens apparell. The spirits of the aire will mix themselues with thunder & lightening, and so infect the Clime where they raise any tempest, that suddenlie great mortalitie shall ensue to the inhabitants from the infectious vapors which arise from their motions: of such S. *Iohn* maketh mention in the 9. of the Apocalips: their patron is *Mereris*, whoe beareth chiefe rule about the middle time of the daie. The spirits of the fire haue their mansions vnder regions of the Moon, that whatsoeuer is committed to their charge, they maie there execute, as in their proper consistorie, from whense they cannot start. The spirites of the earth keepe for the most part in Forrests and woods, and doo hunters much noiance, & sometime in the broade fieldes where they lead trauellers out of the right waie, or fright men with deformed apparitions, or make them run mad through excessiue melancholie lik *Aiax Telamonius*, & so proue hurtfull to themselues, and dangerous to others: of this number the chiefe are *Saniaab* and *Achymael* spirits of the east, / [H3 that haue no power to do anie great harme, by reason of the vnconstancie of their affections. The vnder-earth spirits, are such as lurke in dens & little cauerns of the earth, and hollow creuises of mountaines, that they maie diue into the bowels of the earth at their pleasure: these dig mettals, and watch treasures, which they continuallie transport from place to place, that none should haue vse of them: they raise winds that vomit flames, and shake the foundation of buildings, they dance in rounds in pleasant launds, and greene medowes, with noises of musicke and minstrelsie, & vanish awaie when anie comes neere them: they will take vpon them anie similitude but of a woman, and terrifie men in the likenesse of dead mens ghostes in the night time: and of this qualitie and condition the Necromancers hold *Gaziel*, *Fegor*, and *Anarazel*, Southern spirits to be. Besides, there are yet remaining certeine lieng spirits, (whoe, although all bee giuen to lie by nature) yet are they more prone to that vice, than the rest, being named *Pythonists*, of whome *Apollo* comes to be called *Pytheus*: they haue a prince as well as other spirits, of whom mention is made in the 3. booke of kings, when he saith he will be a lieng spirit in the mouth of all *Ahabs* prophets: from which those spirits of iniquitie do little differ, which are called the vessels of wrath, that assist *Belial* (whom they interpret a spirit without yoke or controuler) in all damnable deuises and inuentions. *Plato* reports them to be such as first deuised cards and dice, and I am in the mind, that the Monke was of the same order, that found out the vse of Gunpouder, and the engins of war therto belonging. Those that write of these matters, call this *Belial Chodar* of the East, that hath all witches & coniurors spirits vnder his iurisdiction, & giues them leaue to helpe Iuglers in their tricks, & *Simon Magus* to doo miracles; alwaies prouided they bring a soule home to their Maister for his hire. Yet are not these all, for there are spirits called spies & tale carriers, obedient to *Ascaroth*, whom the Greeks call *Daimona*, and *S. Iohn The accuser of the brethren:* also tempters, whoe for their interrupting vs in al our good actions, are cald our euil Angels. Aboue all thinges they hate the light and reioyce in darkenesse, disquieting men maliciouslie in the night and somtimes hurt them by pinching them or blasting them as they sleep / but they are [H3v not so much to be dreaded as other spirits, bicause if a man speak to them, they flee awaie and will not abide. Such a spirit *Plinius Secundus* telleth of, that vsed to haunt a goodlie house in *Athens* that *Athenadorus* hired; and such another *Suetonius* describeth to haue long houered in *Lamianus* Garden wher *Caligula* lay buried, who for bicause he was onlie couered with a few clods, and vnreuerentlie thrown amongst the weeds, he meruelouslie disturbed the owners of the garden, & woulde not let them rest in their beds, till by his Sisters returned from banishment, he was taken vp, and intoombed solemnlie. *Pausanias* auoucheth (amongst other experiments) that a certain spirit called *Zazilus* doth feed vpon dead mens corses, that are not deeplie interred in the earth as they ought: which to confirme, there is a wonderfull accident set downe in the Danish history of *Asuitus* and *Asmundus*, who being two famous friends (well knowne in those parts) vowd one to another, that which of them two out liued the other, should be buried aliue with his friende that first died. In short space *Asuitus* fell sick and yeelded to nature, *Asmundus* compelled by the oath of his friendship, tooke none but his horsse and his dog with him, and transported the dead bodie into a vast caue vnder the earth, & there determined (hauing victualed himselfe for a long time) to finish his daies in darknesse, and neuer depart from him that he loued so deerelie. Thus shut vp and inclosed in the bowels of the earth, it hapened *Eritus* K. of *Sweueland* to passe that waie with his armie not full two months after, who comming to the toomb of *Asuitus*, & suspecting it a place where tresure was hidden, caused his Pioners with their spades and mattockes to dig it vp: where vpon was discouered the lothsome bodie of *Asmundus*, all to besmeared with dead mens filth, & his visage most vglie and fearefull; which imbrued with congeald blood, and eaten & torn like a raw vlcer, made him so gastlie to behold, that all the beholders were afrighted. He seeing himselfe restord to light, and so manie amazed men stand about him, resolued their vncertain perplexity in these terms. Why stand you astonisht at my vnusual deformities? when no liuing man conuerseth with the dead, but is thus disfigured. But other causes haue effected this change in mee: for I know not what audacious spirit sent by *Gorgon* from the / deep, hath [H4 not onelie most rauenously deuoured my horse & my dog, but also hath laid his hungrie pawes vpon me, and tering downe my cheekes as you see, hath likewise rent awaie one of mine eares. Hense is it that my mangled shape seems so monstrous, and my humane image obscured with gore in this wise. Yet scaped not this fell Harpie from me vnreuenged: for as he assailde me, I raught his head from his shoulders, and sheathd my sword in his bodie. Haue spirits their visible bodies saide I, that may be toucht, wounded, or pierst? Beleeue me, I neuer heard that in my life before this. Why quoth he, although in their proper essence they are creatures incorporall, yet can they take on them the induments of anie liuing bodie what soeuer, & transform themselues into all kind of shapes, wherby they maie more easilie deceiue our shallow wits and senses. So testifies *Basilius* that they can put on a material forme when they list. *Socrates* affirmeth that his *Dæmon* did oftentimes talke with him, and that he saw him and felt him manie times. But *Marcus Cherronesius* (a wonderfull discouerer of Diuels) writeth, that those bodies which they assume, are distinguisht by no difference of sex, bicause they are simple, and the discernance of sex belongs to bodies compound: yet are they flexible, motiue, and apt for any configuration, but not all of them alike: for the spirits of the Fire and Aire haue this power aboue the rest. The spirits of the water haue slow bodies resembling birdes & women, of which kind the *Naiades* & *Nereieds* are much celebrated amongst Poets. Neuerthelesse, how euer they are restrained to their seuerall similitudes, it is certeine that all of them desire no forme or figure so muche, as the likenesse of a man, and doo thinke themselues in heauen, when they are infeoft in that hue: wherefore I know no other reason but this, that man is the neerest representation to God, insomuch as the scripture saith, *He made man after his own likenesse and image:* and they affecting by reason of their pride, to be as like God as they may, contend most seriouslie to shroud themselues vnder that habit. But I pray tell me this, whether are there (as *Porphirius* holdeth) good Spirits as well as euill. Naie certeinlie (quoth he) we are all euill, let *Porphirius*, *Proclus*, *Apuleius*, or the *Platonists* dispute to the contrarie as long as they will, which I / will confirm to thy [H4v capacitie by the names that are euerie wher giuen vs in the Scripture, for the diuell which is the *Summum genus* to vs all, is called *Diabolus quasi deorsum ruens*, that is to say falling downeward, as he that aspiring too high, was thrown from the top of felicitie to the lowest pit of despaire: and sathan, that is to saie, an Aduersarie, who for the corruption of his malice, opposeth himselfe euer against God, whoe is the chiefest good. In *Iob*, *Behemoth* and *Leuiathan*, and in the 9. of the *Apocalips*, *Apolyon*, that is to saie, a Subuerter: bicause the foundation of those vertues, which our high Maker hath planted in our soules; he vndermineth and subuerteth. A serpent for his pojsoning, a Lyon for his deuouring: a furnace, for that by his malice the Elect are tried, who are vessels of wrath and saluation. In *Esay*, a Syren, a Lamia, a Scrich-oule, an Estridge. In the Psalmes, an Adder, a Basiliske, a Dragon. And lastlie, in the Gospell, Mammon, Prince of this world, and the Gouernour of darknes: so that by the whole course of condemning names that are giuen vs, and no one instance of anie fauourable tytle bestowed vpon vs, I positiuelie set downe that all spirits are euill. Now, whereas the Diuines attribute vnto vs these good and euill spirits, the good to guide vs from euil, and the euill to draw vs from goodnesse, they are not called spirits but Angels, of which sort was *Raphaell*, the good Angell of *Tobias*, who exilde the euill spirit *Asmodius* into the desart of *Aegypt*, that he might be the more secure from his temptation. Since we haue entred thus far into the diuels commonwealth, I beseech you certifie me thus much, whether haue they power to hurt granted them from God, or from themselues; can they hurt as much as they wil. Not so quoth hee, for although that diuels be most mightie spirites, yet can they not hurt but permissiuelie, or by some speciall dispensation: as when a man is faln into the state of an out-law, the Law dispenseth with them that kill him, & the Prince excludes him from the protection of a subiect, so, when a man is a relaps from GOD and his Lawes, God withdrawes his prouidence from watching ouer him, and authoriseth the deuil as his instrument, to assault him and torment him, so that whatsoeuer he dooth, is *Limitata potestate*, as one saithe: insomuche as a haire cannot fall from our / [11 heades, without the will of our heauenlie Father. The Diuell could not deceiue *Achabs* prophets til he was licensed by God, nor exercise his tyranie ouer *Iob* till he had giuen him commission, nor enter into the heard of swine til Christ bad them goe. Therefore need you not feare the diuell any whit as long as you are in the fauor of God, who raineth him so straight, that except he let him loose he can doo nothing. This man like proportion which I now retaine, is but a thinge of suffrance granted vnto me to plague such men as hunt after strife, and are delighted with variance. It may be so very well, but whether haue you that skill to foretell thinges to come, that is ascribed vnto you? We haue (quoth he) sometimes, not that we are priuie to the eternall counsell of god, but for that by the sense of our ayrie bodies we haue a more refined faculty of forseeing, than men possibly can haue, that are chained to such heauie earthlie moulder; or else for that by the incomparable pernicitie of those ayrie bodies, we not onely out-strip the swiftnes of men, beasts & birds, whereby we may be able to attain to the knowledge of thinges sooner, than those that by the dulnes of their earthlie sense come a great waie behind vs. Hervnto may we adioine our long experience in the course of things from the begining of the world, which men want and therfore cannot haue that deepe coniecture that we haue. Nor is our knowledge any more than coniecture: for prescience only belongeth to God, & that gesse that we haue, proceedeth from the compared disposition of heauenly and earthlie bodies, by whose long obserued temperature, we doo diuine manie times, as it happens, & therefore doo we take vpon vs to prophecy, that we may purchase estimation to our names, and bringe men in admiration with that we doo, and so be counted for Gods. The myracles wee work, are partly contriued by illusion, and partly assisted by that supernatural skil we haue in the experience of nature aboue all other Creatures. But against these illusions of your subtletie & vain terrors you inflict, what is our cheefe refuge? I shall be accounted a foolishe Diuell anon, if I bewray the secretes of our kingdome, as I haue begun: yet speak I no more than learned Clarkes haue written, and asmuch as they haue set downe will I shew thee. *Origin* in his treatise against *Celsus* saith, there is nothing better for him / that is vexed with [I1v] spirites, then the naming of *Iesu*, the true God, for he auoucheth, he hath seene diuers driuen out of mens bodies by that means. *Athanasius* in his booke *De varijs questionibus* saith, The presentest remedie againste the inuasion of euill spirits, is the beginning of the 67. Psalme, *Exurgat Deus, & dissipentur inimici eius*. *Cyprian* counsels men to adiure spirites only by the name of the true God. Some hold that fire is a preseruatiue for this purpose, because when any spirit appeareth, the lights by little and little, go out as it were of their own accord, and the tapers are by degrees extinguisht. Others by inuocating vpon God, by the name of *Vehiculum ignis superioris*, and often rehearsing the Articles of our faith. A third sort are perswaded that the brandishing of swords is good for this purpose, because *Homer* faineth, that *Vlisses* sacrificing to his mother, wafted his sworde in the aire to chase the spirits from the blood of the sacrifice. And *Sybylla* conducting *Aeneas* to hell begins hir charmes in this sort.

Procul, O procul, este prophani:
Tuque invande viam, vaginaque eripe ferrum.

Philostratus reporteth that he and his companions meeting that Diuell which Artistes entitle *Apolonius* as they came one night from banquetting, with such terms as he is curst in holy writ, they made him run awaie howling. Manie in this case extoll perfume of *Calamentum pæonia, Menta palma Christi*, and *Appius*. A number prefer the carying of red Corrall about them, or of *Arthemisia hypericon, Ruta verbena*: and to this effect manie doo vse the iyngling of keyes, the sound of the harp, and the clashing of armor. Some of old time put great superstition in characters, curiously engraued in their *Pentagonon*, but they are all vaine, & will doo no good, if they be otherwise vsed than as signes of couenant betweene the diuell and them. Nor doo I

affirme al the rest to bee vnfallible prescriptions, though sometime they haue their vse: but that the onelie assured way to resist their attempts is prayer and faith, gainst which all the diuells in hell cannot preuaile. Inough gentle spirit I will importune thee no further, but commit this Supplication to thy care: which if thou deliuer accordinglie, thou shalt at thy returne haue more of my custome: for by that time I wil haue finished certain letters to diuers Orators & Poets, disperced in your dominions. That / as occation shal serue, [12
but nowe I must take leaue of you, for it is Terme time, and I haue some busines. A Gentleman (a frend of mine that I neuer saw before) staies for me, and is like to be vndoone if I come not in to beare witnesse on his side: wherefore *Bazilez manus*, till our next meeting.

GEntle Reader *tandem aliquando*, I am at leasure to talke to thee. I dare say, thou hast cald me a hundred times dolt for this senseles discourse: it is no matter, thou dost but as I haue doone by a number in my dayes. For who can abide a scuruie pedling Poet to plucke a man by the sleeue at euerie third step in *Paules* Churchyard, & when he comes in to seruey his wares, theres nothing but purgations and vomits wrapt vppe in wast paper. It were verie good the dog whipper in *Paules* would haue a care of this in his vnsauery visitation euerie Saterday: for it is dangerous for suche of the Queenes liedge people, as shall take a viewe of them fasting.

Looke to it you Booksellers and Stationers, and let not your shops be infected with any such goose gyblets or stinking garbadge, as the Iygs of newsmongers, and especiallie such of you as frequent Westminster hall, let them be circumspect what dunghill papers they bring thither: for one bad pamphlet is enough to raise a damp that may poison a whole Tearme, or at the least a number of poore Clyents that haue no money to preuent ill aire by breaking their fasts ere they come thither. Not a base Inck-dropper or scuruy plodder at *Nouerint*, but nailes his asses eares on euerie post and comes off with long *Circumquaque* to the Gentleman Readers, yea the most excrementorie dishlickers of learning are growne so valiant in impudencie, that now they set vp their faces (like Turks) of gray paper to be spet at for siluer games in Finsburie fields. Whilst I am thus talking, me thinks I heare one say, What a fop is this he entitles his booke *A Supplication to the Diuell*, and doth nothing but raile on ideots, and tels a storie of the nature of Spirits. Haue patience good sir, and weele come to you by and by. Is it my Title you find fault with? Why, haue you not seen a Towne surnamed by the principall house in the towne, or a Nobleman deriue his Baronrie from a little village where he hath least land? So fareth it by me in christning of my Booke. / But some will obiect, whereto [I2v tends this discourse of diuels, or how is it induced? Forsooth, if thou wilt needs know my reson, this it is. I bring *Pierce Penilesse* to question with the diuel, as a yoong nouice would talke with a great trauailer: who carrieng an Englishmans appetite to enquire of news, will be sure to make what vse of him he maie, and not leaue anie thing vnaskt, that he can resolue him of. If then the diuell be tedious in discoursing, impute it to *Pierce Penilesse*, that was importunate in demanding; or if I haue not made him so secret or subtill in his Art, as Diuels are woont, let that of *Lactantius* bee mine excuse *lib*. 2. *chap*. 16. *de Origenis errore*, where he saith, the diuels haue no power to lie to a iust manne and if they adiure them by the maiestie of the high God, they will not onlie confesse themselues to be Diuels, but also tell their names as they are. *Deus bone*, what a vaine am I fallen into? what, an Epistle to the Readers in the end of thy booke? Out vppon thee for an arrent blocke, where learndst thou that wit? O sir, holde your peace: a fellow neuer comes to his answere before the offence be committed. Wherfore if I in the beginning of my Book should haue come off with a long Apologie to excuse my selfe, it were all one, as if a theefe going to steale a horse, should deuise by the waie as he went, what to speake when he came at the gallows. Here is a crosse waie, and I thinke it good heere to part. Farwell, farewell, good Parenthesis, and commende mee to Ladie Vanitie thy mistres. Now *Pierce peniles* if for a parting blow thou hast ere a tricke in thy budget more then ordinarie bee not daintie of it, for a good Patron will pay for all. I where is he? *Promissis quilibet diues esse Potest.* But cap and thankes is all our Courtiers payment: wherefore I would counsell my frends to be more considerate in their Dedications, and not cast away so many months labour on a clown that knowes not how to vse a Scholer: for what reason haue I to bestow any wit on him, that wil bestow none of his wealth vpon me. Alas, it is easie for a goodlie tall fellow that shineth in his silkes, to come and out face a poore simple Pedant in a thred bare cloake, and tell him his booke is prety, but at this time he is not prouided for him: marrie about twoe or three daies hence if he come that waie, his Page shall say he is not within, or else he is so busie with my L. How-call-ye-him, and my L. What-call-ye-him, that / he may not be [I3 spoken withall. These are the common courses of the world, which euerie man priuatlie murmurs at but none dares openlie vpbraid, bicause all Artists for the most part are base minded and like the *Indians*, that haue store of gold & pretious stones at command, yet are ignorant of their value, & therfore let the Spaniards, the Englishmen, and euerie one loade their ships without molestation. So they enioying and possessing the puritie of knowledge (a treasure farre richer than the Indian Mines) let euerie proude *Thraso* be partaker of their perfections, repaieng them no profit: and gylde himselfe with the titles they giue him, when he wil scarse returne them a good word for their labor: giue an Ape but a nut, & he will look your head for it; or a dog a bone, and hele wag his taile: but giue me one of my yoong Maisters a booke, and he will put of his hat & blush, and so go his waie: yes, now I remember me I lie, for I know him that had thanks for three yeares worke, and a gentleman that bestowed much cost in refining of musicke, and had scarse Fidlers wages for his labor. We want an *Aretine* here among vs, that might strip these golden asses out of their gaie trappings, and after he had ridden them to death with railing, leaue them on the dunghill for carion. But I will write to his ghost by my carrier, and I hope hele repaire his whip, and vse it against our English Peacockes, that painting themselues with church spoils, like mightie mens sepulchers, haue nothing but Atheisme, schisme, hypocrisie, & vainglory, like rotten bones lie lurking within them. O how my soule abhors these buckram giants, that hauing an outwarde face of honor set vppon them by flaterrs and parasites, haue their inward thoughtes stuft with strawe and feathers, if they were narrowelie sifted. Far be it bright stars of Nobilitie, and glistring attendants on the true *Diana*, that this my speech shoulde be anie way iniurious to your glorious magnificence: for in you liue those sparks of *Augustus* liberalitie, that neuer sent anie awaie emptie: & Science seauenfold throne well nigh ruined by ryot and auarice, is mightilie supported by your plentifull larges, which makes Poets to sing such goodlie himnes of your praise, as no enuious posteritie may forget. But from generall fame, let me digres to my priuate experience, and with a toong vnworthy to / name a [I3v name of such worthines, affectionatelie emblason to the eies that woonder, the matchlesse image of Honor, and magnificent rewarder of vertue, *Ioues Eagle-borne Ganimed*, thrice noble *Amyntas*. In whose high spirit, such a Deitie of wisdom appeereth, that if *Homer* were to write his *Odissea* new (where vnder the person of *Vlysses* he describeth a singular man of perfection, in whom all ornaments both of peace and warre are assembled in the height of their excelence) he need no other instanc to augment his conceipt, than the rare carriage of his honorable minde. Manye writers and good wits, are giuen to commend their patrons and Benefactors, some for prowesse, some for policie, others for the glorie of their Ancestrie and exceeding bountie and liberalitie: but if my vnable pen should euer enterprise such a continuate taske of praise, I woulde embowell a number of those wind puft bladders, and disfurnish their bald-pates of the periwigs Poets haue lent them, that so I might restore glorie to his right inheritance, and these stoln Titles to their true owners: which if it would so fall out, (as time maie worke all thinges) the aspiring nettles with their shadie toppes shal no longer ouer-dreep the best hearbs, or keep them from the smiling aspect of the Sunn, that liue & thriue by his comfortable beames, none but Desert should sit in Fames grace, none but *Hector* be remembred in the chronicles of Prowesse, none but thou most curteous *Amyntas* be the second misticall argument of the knight of the Red-crosse.

Oh decus atque æui gloria summa tui.

And heere (heauenlie *Spencer*) I am most highlie to acuse thee of forgetfulnes, that in that honourable catalogue of our English *Heroes*, which insueth the conclusion of thy famous Fairie Queene, thou wouldst let so speciall a piller of Nobilitie passe vnsaluted. The verie thought of his far deriued discent, & extraordinarie parts wherewith he astonieth the world, and drawes all harts to his loue, would haue inspired thy forewearied Muse with new furie to proceede to the next triumphs of thy statelie Goddesse, but as I in fauor of so rare a scholler, suppose with this counsell he refraind his mention in this first part, that he might with full saile proceed to his due commendations in the second. Of this occasion long since I happened to frame a son- / net which being wholie intended to [14
the reuerence of this renoumed Lord, (to whom I owe all the vtmoste powers of my loue and dutie) I meante heere for variety of stile to insert.

Perusing yesternight with idle eyes,
The Fairy Singers stately tuned verse:
And viewing after Chap-mens wonted guise,
What strange contents the title did rehearse.
I streight leapt ouer to the latter end,
Where like the queint Comædians of our time,
That when their Play is doone do fal to ryme,
I found short lines, to sundry Nobles pend.
Whom he as speciall Mirrours singled fourth,
To be the Patrons of his Poetry;
I read them all, and reuerenc't their worth,
Yet wondred he left out thy memory.
But therefore gest I he supprest thy name,
Because few words might not cõprise thy fame.

Beare with me gentle Poet, though I conceiue not aright of thy purpose, or be too inquisitiue into the intent of thy obliuion: for how euer my coniecture may misse the cushion, yet shal my speech sauour of friendship, though it be not alied to iudgement.

Tantum hoc molior, in this short digression, to acquaint our countreymen that liue out of the Eccho of the Court, with a common knowledge of his inualuable vertues, and shew my selfe thankfull (in some part) for benefits receiued: which since words may not counteruaile, that are the vsuall lip labour of euerie idle discourser, I conclude with that of *Ouid:*

Accipe per longos tibi qui deseruiat annos,
Accipe qui pura nouit amare fide.

And if my zeale and duty (though all to meane to please) may by any industrie, be reformed to your gratious liking, I submit the simplicitie of my indeuours to your seruice, which is, all my performance may profer, or my abilitie performe.

Præbeat Alcinoi poma benignus ager,
Officium pauper numeret studiumque fidemque.

And so I breake off this endlesse argument of speech abruptlie.

FINIS

ERRATA

The following emendations have been made in the text of the original:—

Page	Line		In the Original reads:
5	10	'Earely'	'Eraely'
7	1	'Rymes'	'Bymes'
7	Sidenote		'Scribimus iuderi doctiqui/ poequiæa passim.'
8	2	'of *Tom*'	'*Tom*'
8	8	'lookes?'	'lookes.'
13	25	'backe'	'backt'
15	26	'shape'	'shame'
15	29	'trade'	'crade'
18	8	'imprison-ment),'	'imprison-ment,'
18	27	'there:'	'there?'
21	21	'pinch-fart penie-father'	'pinch fart-penietather.'
21	23	'presents).'	'presents.'
22	1	'(that'	'that'
22	29	'degree;'	'degree?'
26	27	'soyle. It'	'soyle It'
30	26	'*Cæsar*'	'*Cœsar*'
39	8	'his trade,'	'his, trade'
45	1	'Dutch-butter'	'Dutch-bntter'
46	16	'end. His'	'end His'
47	6	'with'	'wit'
47	7	'eve'	'hve'
48	16	'all'	'all all'
57	4	'Sermon. Prooue'	'Sermon, Prooue'
57	27	'is'	'in'
58	3	'aboue'	'about'
59	16	'world. What'	'world What'
63	8	'lyes'	'lyers'
64	14	'way. Why'	'way, Why'

Page	Line		In the Original reads:
68	7	'feasts. Much'	'feasts, Much'
75	4	'neere'	'neeer'
77	Sidenote	'against drinking'	'aȝainst driuking'
78	10	'iustified'	'instified'
78	Sidenote	'priuat'	'eriuat'
79	23	'lumpish'	'bumpish'
80	16	'note'	'nose'
81	27	'Box-keeper'	'Bax-keeper'
85	21	'inuasion. There'	'inuasion, There'
89	Sidenote	'Players'	'dlayers'
89	9	'come'	'came'
90	7	'mischeife.'	'mischiefe,'
91	26	'(as'	')as'
98	29	'*Grathon-icall*'	'*Guathon-icall*'
101	14	'satisfied;'	'satisfied?'
107	12	'but yet'	'but * yet'
107	23	'Canonical'	'Canonic al'
109	29	'*homini*'	'*bomini*'
111	11	'darkness. The'	'darkness, The'
111	20	'contayneth'	'contayueth'
119	7	'*Suetonius*'	'*Suctonius*'
121	21	'*Dæmon*'	'*Danon*'
122	5	'Poets'	'Poete'
131	8	'speake'	'spake'
134	11	'excelence)'	'excelence'
137	6	'seruice'	'sernice'

100179507